"What a great book to get you off on the right foot for e-learning! I found it easy to read, eminently practical, and filled with good sense and useful tools. It confirms a lot of what I have experienced in creating e-learning and offers the kind of warnings I wish others would make. I will re⋯ ⋯nd clients."

⋯ld D. Stolovitch,
⋯linical professor,
⋯cipal, Harold D.
⋯nance Solutions

"Not on⋯ ⋯riven from the pers⋯ ⋯l the *ABCs of e-Learnir⋯* ⋯l learning is much le⋯ ⋯, clear, and sensitive⋯ —Gilly Salmon,
⋯r of *E-moderating*

"e-Lear⋯ ⋯ations, but it remains⋯ ⋯tives, and train- ers. Bro⋯ ⋯ok describes e-learnir⋯ ⋯ue and how to achieve⋯ ⋯is about, the *ABCs of*⋯ —Jay Cross,
⋯Learning Forum

"The *Al*⋯ ⋯actual imple- mentatio⋯ ⋯ge of e-learning activitie⋯ ⋯of informal as well as f⋯ ⋯n to make this book sta⋯ ⋯pertinent and useful. If you are going to buy one book on e-learning, this is the one!"

—Kevin Wheeler, president,
Global Learning Resources Forum

"The author exhibits a combination of objectivity and the ability to write lucidly without the crutch of jargon and buzzwords. Both are welcome. e-Learning has been damaged by hype." —Bill Ellet, editor, *Training Media Review*

"A must read for anyone working with e-learning or considering it. e-Learning is part of the self-service model that business is moving to. Fits the style of today's management and individual behaviors."
—Robert Gunn,
group chief operating officer, Royal & Sun Alliance
Insurance Group plc, Worldwide Operations

"An enlightening insight into e-learning and the necessary implementation strategies for organizations. This book provides an invaluable guide derived from real-life experiences and is ideal for academic travelers on the e-learning road." —Dr. Jo Hamilton-Jones,
senior lecturer in information technology,
University College Worcester, U.K.

"Finally a book that helps demystify the confusion surrounding the implementation of e-learning strategies. Insightful and straightforward, Brooke Broadbent's experience as a successful practitioner captures the key issues that need to be considered for effective e-learning initiatives. The *ABC's of e-Learning* is a must have for every training professional's resource library." —Michael Nolan, president, Friesen, FKA

"Competitive differentiation. Increased customer loyalty. Business transformation. Accelerated product launches. Tangible results like these are achieved only when you invest in your human enterprise. Broadbent's book tells you how to make those investments wisely." —Greg Priest,
CEO, SmartForce

ABCs of e-Learning

Reaping the Benefits and Avoiding the Pitfalls

Brooke Broadbent

ASTD
*Linking People,
Learning & Performance*

JOSSEY-BASS/PFEIFFER
A Wiley Company
www.pfeiffer.com

Published by

JOSSEY-BASS/PFEIFFER

A Wiley Company
989 Market Street
San Francisco, CA 94103-1741
415.433.1740; Fax 415.433.0499
800.274.4434; Fax 800.569.0443

www.pfeiffer.com

ASTD

Linking People,
Learning & Performance

1640 King Street   Box 1443
Alexandria, VA 22313-2043   USA

Tel *800.628.2783   703.683.8100*
Fax *703.683.8103*

www.astd.org

Copyright © 2002 by ASTD.
Jossey-Bass/Pfeiffer is a registered trademark of Jossey-Bass Inc., A Wiley Company.
ISBN: 0-7879-5910-3
Library of Congress Catalog Card Number 2002000939

Library of Congress Cataloging-in-Publication Data

Broadbent, Brooke.
  ABCs of e-learning : reaping the benefits and avoiding the
pitfalls / Brooke Broadbent.
    p. cm.
  Includes bibliographical references and index.
  ISBN 0-7879-5910-3 (alk. paper)
  1. Internet in education. 2. Computer-assisted instruction.
3. Employees—Training of—Computer-assisted instruction.
I.Title.
LB1044.87 .B75 2002
371.33'4—dc21   2002000939

Jossey-Bass also publishes its books in a variety of electronic formats. Some content that appears in print may not be available in electronic books.

No part of this publication may be reproduced, stored in a retrieval system, or transmitted in any form or by any means, electronic, mechanical, photocopying, recording, scanning, or otherwise, except as permitted under Sections 107 or 108 of the 1976 United States Copyright Act, without either the prior written permission of the Publisher or authorization through payment of the appropriate per-copy fee to the Copyright Clearance Center, 222 Rosewood Drive, Danvers, MA 01923, (978) 750-8400, fax (978) 750-4744. Requests to the Publisher for permission should be addressed to the Permissions Department, John Wiley & Sons, Inc., 605 Third Avenue, New York, NY 10158-0012, (212) 850-6011, fax (212) 850-6008, e-mail: permreq@wiley.com.

Printed in the United States of America

We at Jossey-Bass strive to use the most environmentally sensitive paper stocks available to us. Our publications are printed on acid-free recycled stock whenever possible, and our paper always meets or exceeds minimum GPO and EPA requirements.

Acquiring Editor: Josh Blatter
Director of Development: Kathleen Dolan Davies
Developmental Editor: Leslie Stephen
Editor: Rebecca Taff
Senior Production Editor: Dawn Kilgore
Manufacturing Supervisor: Becky Carreño
Cover Design: Bruce Lundquist
Illustrations: Lotus Art

Printing 10   9   8   7   6   5   4   3   2   1

DEDICATION

To an army of e-learning students, early adopters, who were patient with the initial modest results. To e-learning leaders, using their brains, their hearts, and their courage, who persevered and are improving e-learning products and services. Working together, they are moving e-learning forward.

About ASTD

ASTD is the world's leading association of workplace learning and performance professionals, forming a world-class community of practice. ASTD's
70,000 members come from more than one hundred countries and 15,000
organizations, multinational corporations, medium-sized and small businesses,
government, academia, consulting firms, and product and service suppliers.

Started in 1944 as the American Society of Training Directors, ASTD is now
a global force, widening the industry's focus to connect learning and performance to measurable results, and is a sought-after voice on critical public
policy issues.

For more information, visit www.astd.org or call 800.628.8723 (International,
703.683.8100).

CONTENTS

TABLES AND FIGURES

FOREWORD

As we enter the 21st Century, the use of e-learning is revolutionizing how people obtain training. Multimedia training programs are now increasingly available on CD-ROM or through the Internet or company-sponsored intranets (internal Web sites). The advantage of computer technology is the ability to provide more training, delivered sooner, in more places, and potentially at a lower cost than traditional classroom-based instruction. The value of e-learning is enhanced when it is designed for maximum interactivity. Straightforward presentation of information, even when it is "hypertext" format and replete with visual graphics, provides a limited learning experience. However, questions, case problems, and simulations and interactive exercises alter the quality of learning. Such activities can be built into e-learning tools via user input options that enable learners to "talk" to the material. And on the social side of learning, it is also possible to bring together, both face-to-face and virtually, people who have experienced the same e-learning activities and give them group activities to reinforce what they have learned individually.

What really gives e-learning potential as an active learning experience is the fact that the learner can make his or her own decisions about how to learn the material. Classroom-based instruction is linear. A participant learns point A before point B. Nonlinear learning is the hallmark of e-learning. A participant can repeat material, skip material, and, in fact, begin and end whenever he or she wants. Simply creating a techno version of a linear lecture would be a waste of the learners' time.

Currently, the effectiveness of e-learning is being hotly debated. How well can an interactive CD-ROM, for instance, teach and have the learner practice interpersonal behaviors used in areas such as presentations, coaching sessions, and sales calls? Such skill-based learning includes input of the knowledge necessary to perform the skill, demonstration, preparation, practice application, feedback, and re-application. Most critical are the quality and delivery of the coaching/feedback and of the re-application. Some say that it's tough for technology to deliver these steps as well as good, old-fashioned human beings can—at least for now.

Distance learning is a way to provide training when trainer and participants are not at the same site nor necessarily interacting at the same time. It can be accomplished through both video conferencing and computer conferencing. Once again, the value of distance learning is diminished when the learning process is one-way—with a "talking head" lecturing on TV or an online instructor filling computer screens with endless information. Fortunately, distance educators are becoming mindful of this. For example, the 12th Annual Conference on Distance Teaching and Learning was devoted to "Designing for Active Learning." Much research was presented that tested the hypothesis: "Whatever can be done in a classroom can be done in a distance learning classroom." Experimentation in fostering active learning online, creating team learning experiences for remote students, electronic journaling, and collaborative computer-mediated conferencing is ongoing and all seem possible in the future.

In the *ABCs of e-Learning,* we are taken back to the basics—to fundamental principles of active learning. e-Learning brings new opportunities, new challenges, new benefits, and new pitfalls. In the end, the future of e-learning depends on you as instructors, developers, and managers. This book is a great way to get you on the e-learning highway.

—Mel Silberman
Author, *Active Training*

ACKNOWLEDGMENTS

If it takes a village to raise a child, how many people does it take to create a book? The answer, at least for the *ABCs of Learning*, is that it is the product of the tender loving care of my personal e-learning villlage. My village comprised some two hundred people who played a significant role in shaping this book's content. Each one deserves to be acknowledged for the contribution of his or her ideas, experiences, and encouragement.

The idea for the book started with a phone in-radio show that I did in October 1, 1998, with Dave Stephens of the Canadian Broadcasting Corporation. During the hour, all callers spoke enthusiastically about what most people were then calling online learning. They gave new diverse perspectives of online learning from their experiences. I have quoted the callers in text boxes throughout the book. Around the same time, PricewaterhouseCoopers, encouraged me to write a book about e-learning. John Herzog, my partner at PwC, encouraged me in a fatherly way. Colleagues in Canada, the United States, Ireland, and England drew on their diverse experiences to help me write an article about change management and e-learning that is embedded in this book.

I spoke at conferences about e-learning and attended sessions by other experts in the field. I participated in over a dozen conferences and picked up many ideas about e-learning from the experience of other presenters and from the questions and comments of participants who attended sessions I gave across North America. Thanks to organizers of e-learning conferences, I was able to expand my knowledge and contacts in the e-learning domain, test out my ideas, and expand my global e-learning village.

I am also grateful to publishers that gave me an opportunity to write about e-learning. The articles I wrote provided paths that this book follows. In addition to regular columns in *e-Learning Magazine* and the *Training Report,* I wrote articles for *Training and Development.* I also wrote several book reviews about e-learning for various ASTD publications. Excellent books by Bill Horton and Marc Rosenberg helped support ideas that I was developing and gave a boost in my thinking. I also appreciate the opportunity to publish e-learning articles in anthologies from Jossey-Bass, ASTD, and McGraw-Hill.

I met at the village coffee shop, as it were, with Nancy Olsen and Marc Morrow of the American Society for Training and Development. This book started to take shape in our discussions some three years ago. Based on his experience working with ASTD members, Mark advised me to provide practical e-learning advice to instructors, developers, and managers of e-learning. Mark gave me personalized, face-to-face feedback on my first draft. In addition, Paul Candy Yvon Côté, Rob Fonger, and Denis Marcil gave me plenty of feedback and ideas for additional content. Paul, for example shared with me his ideas about starting off on the right foot with an e-learning consultant. His thoughts became a checklist in Chapter Nine.

When Matt Holt of Jossey-Bass invited me to write a book about e-learning, ASTD (where I already had a contract) generously agreed to a co-publishing agreement. Jossey-Bass brought their full resources to the undertaking. They submitted the draft manuscript to three anonymous reviewers who gave me abundant feedback. Under their influence, I included more examples from my consulting experience and added several tools to the manuscript to help people apply the ideas. Editors Kathleen Dolan Davis and Samya Sattar closely followed progress in the book and arranged for the assistance of Leslie Stephen, a developmental editor. Leslie suggested major changes to the flow of the book. Dawn Kilgore and others, including Jin Im, worked behind the scenes to bring the book to maturity.

While writing I continued to do e-learning consulting, working as a subcontractor with Garry DeRose of the College Center of the Finger Lakes, Yvon Côté of Tecsult, and Gina Walker of Harold Stolovitch and Associates. For most of the period I was working with the Canadian Armed Forces, helping them implement e-learning, or what they call distributed learning. I am especially grateful to Dan Hansen for granting me permission to include tools that I developed while consulting with the Canadian Force. My colleagues in the Canadian military contributed to specific chapters. Regan Legassie was the main author of Chapter Three. Ralph Kellett was the main author of Chapter Ten. Yvon Côté, Peter Sabiston, and Elizabeth Syversten-Bitten provided significant input for Chapter Seven. Throughout, Dan Hansen and Liz Allan of the CF were sounding boards with whom I could swap e-learning war stories.

Teaching provided opportunities to test my ideas and learn about students' preoccupations. I'm grateful for the opportunity I was given. Paul Shrivastava of eSocrartes engaged me to teach a course about e-learning. As a result, I was able to use draft chapters of the book with people from three continents. Likewise for Phoenix University. While teaching there, I used snippets from this book with people from North America, Europe, and Australia. Designing and teaching an e-learning consulting course at the master's level for Doug Hamilton at Royal Roads University also provided an opportunity to reflect on e-learning issues and learn about the experiences and concerns of my students.

Every village has its leaders. In villages, people become leaders by helping others. So it is in the e-learning world. I received helping hands from Allison Rossett, Bill Ellet, Bill Horton, Brandon Hall, Diane Gayeski, Elliott Masie, Jay Cross, Kim Kiser, Lance Dublin, Marcia Conner, Mel Silberman, Roger Shank, and Thiagi. They quickly agreed when I asked to quote them. Generous leaders, some of the same people, took the time to read the manuscript and provide endorsements.

Now our village has grown. You've joined. By reading this book you become connected to all of the people listed above—and to all the others who are also reading the book. Together we are getting to know e-learning better. Together we will tame the wild beast that is threatening some of our villages. Some of us have tamed the beast and, like camels, horses, and elephants, all wild beasts at one time, e-learning is serving our villages.

Me. What did I do? I kept the project going through fourteen drafts. I kept my senses turned to my e-learning experiences, extracting the juice for this book. And I'll take the flack for any errors or omissions. In the future, I'll also engage with you if you would like to discuss the book's content. I'm always in a learning mode. Let me know what you are thinking and experiencing about e-learning. Maybe we will co-author a piece one day. Then I can acknowledge you.

Brooke Broadbent
Ottawa, Ontario

INTRODUCTION

Getting on the e-Learning Highway

E-Learning is catching on for enterprise training and education worldwide at all levels. Where do you fit in the e-learning journey? Planning your trip? Already embarked? Well along the way—a true pioneer? Is the trip going well? Or are you lost? Is the road smooth? Or is it bumpy? Too many twists and turns ahead? Wondering about turning around and returning home? Looking for a new roadmap? Need some advice? Thought about asking for directions?

You've come to the right place. This book will help you find the right e-learning path for you and your organization. I'll act as your personal chauffeur, tour guide, and coach—helping you reap the benefits and avoid the pitfalls of e-learning.

> "Information technology is changing the access to knowledge, the process of learning, and the delivery of education and training. Teaching and learning can now take place outside the traditional institutional and workplace-based venues for education and training that are anchored in accreditation and certification and tied to defined skills, jobs, and career paths. Within this new context, the adult who has been an occasional 'student' becomes a continuous 'consumer' of knowledge available worldwide, any time and anywhere. As employees increasingly gain control over their own learning and career development, employers face difficult challenges in training and retaining a workforce with consistent levels of skill."[1]
> —*ASTD and National Governors' Association*
> *Commission on Technology and Adult Learning*

Not sure whether you are even on the right road? Think about the roles of trainers, instructional designers and developers, training managers, consultants, and even line and staff managers today. All are touched by e-learning. Consider, for example, Trina, Don, Manfred, and Lorry and the issues they face in transitioning to e-learning.

Trina is a trainer. She has ten years' experience in the classroom. Her multinational employer is giving serious consideration to getting into e-learning in a big way. Trina wonders what the changes will mean to her career. Trina asks, "How can I prepare for e-learning? Is it for me?"

Don designs and develops learning materials for delivery in the classroom. Don's employer is on the verge of implementing e-learning. Don wonders whether the skills that he used to design, develop, and evaluate classroom training will suffice for e-learning. He knows his way around conventional training but wonders, "Do I have what it takes to become an e-learning instructional designer?"

Manfred heads the HR department for a young manufacturing company. Manfred and several other company leaders have heard that other companies are using e-learning successfully and wonder whether they should go in that direction. His company has experienced some bumpy roads recently with a lack of quality control and trouble with getting products to market on time. "Will e-learning improve the bottom line of the company?" ask Manfred and his management colleagues.

Lorry is an eager, young administrative assistant in a public sector organization. She is fast and accurate with figures and loves the accounting work her job entails. For years she has wondered about taking more accounting courses to take her career more in that direction. Now she wonders whether she should study accounting online.

If you are like Trina, Don, Manfred, or Lorry—an instructor, developer, manager, or learner who needs to make decisions or provide advice about adopting e-learning—you will find this book helpful.

Even if you are not facing an e-learning decision at the moment, it is likely you will soon need to get up to speed on the subject. A long litany of advantages for all types of organizations is driving training and education toward e-learning. Besides the specific advantages for instructors, developers, managers, and learners, there are several mega-advantages:

- The bottom line focus of today's organizations leads managers and training staff to reduce training and education program costs. e-Learning may cost more to develop initially, but it can also save bundles on delivery and overhead by reducing capital expenditure for buildings and the costs of travel and accommodation for business training.
- Increasing numbers of learners in education and business are more and more motivated, independent, and focused. They know they must continue learning or they will fall behind. Many are computer literate and ready for the independent study mode of e-learning. Learners with busy schedules and family responsibilities appreciate the opportunity to study at home or at the office.
- Entrepreneurs look at the forecasts indicating that there will be substantial growth in online learning. e-Learning is touted as a golden opportunity, the answer to downsized staff and shrinking travel budgets.

When the projected surge in technology-driven training hits your organization, you could face difficult questions:

- Is your organization—public, private, or not-for-profit—ready to benefit from new e-learning approaches?
- Are you personally ready to be a pioneer who develops, uses, or manages e-learning?
- What can you—as an instructor, instructional designer, manager, or learner—do to reap the advantages of e-learning innovations?
- Are you ready to help open the new frontier?
- When your organization is faced with a decision about whether to use e-learning, how will it decide?
- What drives decisions like these? Perhaps an influential decision maker read the latest article or advertisement in a management or training publication and convinced top brass that all learning materials should be converted to e-learning immediately, if not sooner.

e-Learning can be an expensive option and it may not be the right one. And *if* it makes sense for your organization to embrace e-learning, what type should it be? What design and delivery strategies would be most effective for your organization? How large an investment of resources will be needed? And how can you prepare to avoid the pitfalls that lie before any organization that decides to adopt an e-learning approach?

You want to make and contribute to reasoned decisions. The purpose of this book is to help you get on the road to making sound decisions about e-learning and to reaping the rewards.

Your Guidebook

ABCs of e-Learning offers insight into four types of e-learning: leader-led, self-paced, performance support tools, and informal learning. The emphasis is on e-learning in the workplace, drawing on my experience as an instructor, developer, and manager of e-learning as well as the insights of other experts and practitioners in the field. The overall approach, planning and implementation frameworks, and step-by-step procedures are meant to be adapted to the situation in your individual organization, whether in the public or private sectors, a business or an educational institution—small, medium, large, or even extra large. The tools, checklists, practical tips, and exercises are designed to help you develop the best approach for your particular situation.

The book provides the background, poses the problems, provides sample answers, and gets you started. You supply the creativity and perseverance to apply what you learn in this book to your situation.

Three Promises

In this never-have-enough-time-to-do-everything era, it is difficult to find time to read, or even skim, a book. I make the following promises to help you spend your time and money wisely:

- *Balanced information for sound decision making.* You'll get balanced information about e-learning, highlighting the benefits and the risks of each stage of program design and delivery. This solid information will help you make sound decisions.
- *Broad perspective.* This book will provide a broad perspective of e-learning with examples from the United States, Canada, and Europe. I'll give you abundant references—a gateway to further exploration for those who wish to go further.

- *Multiple roles.* My advice will focus on the roles of e-learning trainers, developers, managers—and from time to time learners. Many readers may play more than one of the four roles and may not realize when they move from one to another; nevertheless, breaking out the four roles helps us to grasp different, essential aspects of planning, designing, and implementing e-learning strategies.

www.e-learninghub.com

Another way to help you reap the benefits and avoid the pitfalls of e-learning is through the e-learninghub.com Web site operated in connection with this book. The Hub provides continuously updated information on e-learning, including publications, courses, and resources. It contains an easy-to-use search engine that you can use to find articles and other information you need to implement e-learning successfully. The resources section also links you to other Web sites that will help you find additional solid e-learning information.

Getting Started

Eager to start? You may choose to follow the book's logic, starting at the beginning and working your way to the end:

- Part One is a broad introduction to e-learning concepts and terms and an overview of its risks and rewards; it concludes with a chapter with "lessons from the trenches," a compilation of the successful and not-so-successful e-learning experiences of a wide range of organizations.
- Part Two covers the practical aspects of planning and implementing e-learning programs, starting with a systems overview of the process and going through all the design, delivery, and evaluation challenges you are likely to face.
- The last chapter in the book is a summing up and an invitation to think critically about the issues and challenges you will encounter when you begin to put e-learning principles and practices into your organization.
- Finally, there is a glossary of key terms used in this book. You can use it to refresh your memory as you read.

Instead of starting at the beginning and proceeding to the end, you might decide to scan the contents and go directly to the section that seems most relevant to you. If you are an instructor, you may appreciate the story of Vicky in Chapter Eight. Instructional designers might want to go straight to Chapters Four, Five, and Six, which contain a substantial amount of information about designing and developing e-learning. If you want to learn about selecting software, Chapter Seven is a good place to start. Training managers might prefer to go directly to Chapter Nine, which features tips for how to lead e-learning projects.

As you begin, remember the adage "A little learning is a dangerous thing." This book represents "a little learning" in the sense that it is an introduction to a complex, expanding, and evolving field. To situate you, we will explain several roads you can follow and give you tips to help you choose. However, you must finish the job—by selecting what you need from this book, perhaps modifying our tools to suit your situation. Then it's up to you to move forward, avoiding pitfalls and reaping the benefits. You will be able to expand your knowledge and move toward mastery of e-learning by applying the ideas developed in this book and by exploring the abundant e-learning resources suggested throughout.

THE CHALLENGE TO GET IT RIGHT

e-Learning Fundamentals

The Introduction oriented you to this book and to some of the issues faced by e-learning developers, instructors, managers, and learners. Part One is a broad introduction to e-learning. It is designed to familiarize you with e-learning concepts and terms and to give you a sense of the risks and rewards of employing this exciting new method of learning design and delivery. There also are "lessons from the trenches" in the final chapter in this section. These provide opportunities to learn from some of the successful and not-so-successful e-learning experiences of a wide range of organizations.

Specific topics you will find covered in Part One are

- Basic e-learning terms and concepts
- Definitions of four types of e-learning
- Ways to blend the four types of e-learning successfully
- An overview of opportunities and challenges in e-learning today
- Best practices and lessons learned from e-learning pioneers

CHAPTER ONE

KEY CONCEPTS AND TERMS

E-Learning is not just a trendy word. It is a new approach built on what we have learned from developing and instructing with thirty years of computer-based methods and on what we know about how to help people learn. Is e-learning another flavor-of-the-month approach to training and education? No. The concept of e-learning is changing the way we instruct and learn. At the same time, e-learning is evolving, and it is likely that what we call e-learning today will be different in a few years. For example, it may be delivered through wireless devices in the future. Could e-learning fade like videocassettes, audiocassettes, and other training technology? I don't think so, but as the method is absorbed into conventional learning designs through so-called blended learning solutions, the term itself may become extinct.

In this book, the term *e-learning* (electronic learning) refers to training, education, coaching, and information that is delivered digitally. e-Learning may be *synchronous*, meaning that learners and instructors are interacting in real time, or not, in which case the term *asynchronous* applies. e-Learning is normally delivered through a network or via the Internet, but it may also be delivered by CD-ROM, satellite, and even supported by the telephone. In most organizations, personal computers are used to deliver e-learning digitally, but personal digital assistants (PDAs) and other wireless devices are increasingly being used. e-Learning therefore includes such familiar methods as multimedia, CBT (computer-based training), and other forms of technology-assisted learning. The essence of e-learning is that it's digital.

Four Types of e-Learning

The World of e-Terms

e-Learning thought leaders offer a world of definitions, most of which find a new creative meaning for the "e" in e-learning.

Elliott Masie, an e-learning guru, has said that the "e" stands for experience.[1] When e-learning was experiencing an early growth period in 2000 and 2001, vendors and consultants placed definitions on their Web sites. These explanations have since disappeared, but they are helpful to give us some of the perspectives on e-learning. For SmartForce, a leading e-learning vendor, e-learning is "dynamic, collaborative, individual, comprehensive; it happens in real time, and it enables the enterprise. Click2learn.com took a broad, general view, suggesting that e-learning simply refers to the "creation, delivery, and management of training." Cisco tells us that e-learning is "Internet-enabled learning." And for a fun-with-e definition, Eric Parks at ASK International tells us that the e stands for everything, everyone, engaging, and easy.

Each of these definitions has its value. They bring to light the many faces of e-learning. However, they do not reveal the essence of e-learning: *it's digital.*

To further explore the meaning of e-learning, Jay Cross has set up a Web site called The eLearning Jump Page[2] that examines definitions of e-learning and includes links that put you in touch with outstanding e-learning resources.

It seems that everyone from e-learning theorists and practitioners to vendors and learners applies the *term e-learning* to very different methods and products. At the 2001 e-HR Conference, keynote speaker Elliott Masie poked fun at e-learning vendors for saying that they had "B2B, end-to-end, best of breed total solutions."[3] His point was that some vendors were claiming to be all things to all people. (Sometimes it is easier to say that you can do everything than it is to specialize in an area.)

To simplify our discussion, let's say there are four types of e-learning:

1. Informal,
2. Self-paced,
3. Leader-led, and
4. Performance support tools.

In *informal learning,* a learner accesses a Web site or focused online community and finds pertinent information. This type of e-learning is not training because it does not include a formal instructional strategy consisting of a presentation of material, application exercises, and feedback.

Self-paced learning refers to the process whereby learners access computer-based (CBT) or Web-based (WBT) training materials at their own pace, normally on a CD-ROM for CBT or over a network or the Internet for WBT. Learners select what they wish to learn, decide when they will learn it, and set the pace they wish.

Unlike self-paced, *leader-led e-learning* always involves an instructor, coach, or facilitator. There are two basic forms: (1) learners access real-time (synchronous) materials via videoconferencing or an audio or text messaging service such as chat, or (2) learners access delayed materials (asynchronous) through threaded discussions or streamed audio or video.

Performance support tools is our fourth e-learning type. This is an umbrella term for online materials that learners access to gain help in performing a task, normally in software. Performance support tools normally lead the user through the steps required to perform a task.

The four types we are using here closely parallel familiar classifications for conventional training (Table 1.1).

TABLE 1.1. E-LEARNING TYPES AND CONVENTIONAL LEARNING COUNTERPARTS.

e-Learning Type and Examples	Conventional Learning Type and Examples
Informal Learning: a well-designed Web site	*Informal Learning:* books, discussions, articles, ad hoc coaching
Self-Paced: WBT program	*Self-Paced:* self-study manuals
Leader-Led: a facilitated online discussion	*Leader-Led:* workshops, seminars
Performance Support Tools: a wizard to help learn software	*Job Aids:* cheat sheets to remind one how to use software

There also are e-learning hybrids created from combining the four pure types, plus the so-called *blended types,* consisting of conventional *and* e-learning methods.

Informal

People have always learned to do their jobs by informal means. They discuss with colleagues, read articles, peruse files, and use a host of other ways that we tend to take for granted. But, you might object, informal learning is not the domain of trainers; our work is to develop formal training. In my view, it's not that simple. People are now learning to do their jobs, and they always have, through *informal* means. Today those means have expanded to include the Web, organization intranets, discussion groups, and email. What is the role of trainers here?

Typically, folks in the training world focus their attention on *formal learning*. With conventional learning, formal learning means workshops, self-paced manuals, and the like. When it comes to e-learning, examples of formal learning would include online leader-led sessions and self-paced CBT or WBT.

If you are a training professional who believes in a structured approach to learning, you might question the use of terms such as informal learning or unstructured learning. If you are a disciple of the instructional systems design (ISD) school of thinking, you probably think of learning as a formal, structured process. Learning works best, you have been taught, when the designer follows a structured process of needs analysis, development of performance objectives, rigorous development of content, a structured delivery, and evaluation. Informal learning as examined here has none of these qualities of formal learning. Is it effective? Is it worthy of consideration in our scheme of things?

Forms of Informal e-Learning. Stop to reflect for a minute. Think about what you have done in the last few days in your work. Met and discussed ideas? Asked questions? Learned a few pertinent facts about the work you do? Discovered facts about customers, colleagues, or competitors? Conveyed your findings and thoughts in discussions, memoranda, and email messages?

Now for the second step. How much of the knowledge you used above was learned through formal training sessions? Not much, I suspect. Every day you learn critical business information through informal learning—through reading and discussing—not through formal, classroom learning. Perhaps you picked up some of your informal learning from Web sites or Internet discussion groups. If you don't now—you will in the future.

The Web, Internet, and Intranets. With 24/7 information on the Web, informal e-learning opportunities abound. By spanning the globe, each Web site makes its information available any time to everyone who needs it. The intranets in many companies provide similarly powerful resources for informal learning. Collecting knowledge about events, policies, and other business issues—plus managing the knowledge so that people who need it can access it—that's what Web and intranet e-learning resources do well.

A good example of an informal e-learning site is provided by Engines for Education, from Roger Shank and his colleagues at The Institute for the Learning Sciences at Northwestern University. The site offers four access routes to the information. (Different mouse strokes for different folks.) It also provides a one-page complete overview for someone who wants to see the big picture. It is a cleverly hypertexted document to help readers find their way through information about technology-assisted learning.[4] Another good example of an informal learning site is from Kimeiko Hotta,[5] an instructor at Toronto's Seneca College, at her site, www.about.com, Teaching and Learning with Technology. There is plenty of information organized in a way that makes it readily accessible.

Online Discussion Groups. A second informal e-learning resource is the online discussion group. Participants can learn a great deal by formulating and posting queries and by just lurking and observing questions and answers posted by other participants. Some discussion groups archive the replies to questions, and many have a FAQ (frequently asked questions) section where key questions and answers are posted.

How Can I Learn More About Online Discussion Groups?

Over twelve million people subscribe to Topica-hosted newsletters. Topica.com is a free email publishing service serving more than 70,000 individual publishers and delivering 100,000 newsletters on topics as diverse as Java development, bargain shopping, and pointers for working parents.[6]

The following links will help you to set up and facilitate online discussion groups, also known as mailing lists and listservs. Learn how to facilitate discussion groups and e-learning at http://pcbs042.open.ac.uk/gilly/. An online book about how to set up and facilitate mailing lists is at www.idrc.ca/books/848/index_e.html.

Other Terms for Informal Learning. Some training organizations will never subscribe to the term *informal* learning. Some organizations pride themselves on having a structured, systematic approach to learning and any hint of an "informal" approach to learning runs counter to their culture. In these organizations, you might use the terms *push learning* to describe formal learning and *pull learning* to describe informal learning. Informal learning is a pull phenomenon in the sense that learners seek the information they require and find it on the Web or intranet. Push, of course, refers to formal courses that are sent, or pushed, to students.

The term *knowledge management* (KM) is also used to describe informal learning. It is a good descriptor for the framework used for informal learning. The essence of knowledge management—locating, storing, and accessing what KM experts have learned to call explicit (documented knowledge) and tacit information (documented experience)—is also the essence of informal learning. In many organizations, however, it is not appropriate for training professionals to use the term *knowledge management,* as the knowledge management professionals have already built their organizations around the term and implemented their own systems. As a training professional implementing e-learning, the last thing you need is a war with your knowledge management professionals. The obvious solution is to work closely with them. Explain to them what you are doing in the informal e-learning field and seek their collaboration. Knowledge management professionals have experience that can help e-learning succeed. Tap into it!

Self-Paced

In *self-paced* e-learning, the learners themselves determine the speed—and sometimes the sequence—of their progress through a professionally developed training course. Because self-paced courses and materials are designed and developed by training professionals, they are a formal rather than informal method of learning. We are using the term self-paced e-learning to include what many people call WBT, Web-based training. Because of the Web's limitations for data transfer, WBT might not have the capacity to include the sound files and video files that have become associated with CBT. Transferring all your CBT instructional materials to the WBT format could therefore be a step backward, as WBT cannot accommodate all the multimedia features we have come to associate with CBT. Of course, training managers are attracted to WBT because it is distributed over the Web, which means it is easier to disseminate than CBT or a CD-ROM.

As we explained above, CBT is also a type of e-learning, as it includes a learner, content, and technology. Therefore, an organization that commits to e-learning does not need to dispense with CBT, or multimedia, as it is sometimes called.

Figure 1.1 illustrates a course where learners can keep track of what they have studied and what remains to be studied in a self-paced course.[7]

FIGURE 1.1. A WBT PROGRAM ILLUSTRATING SELF-PACED INSTRUCTION.

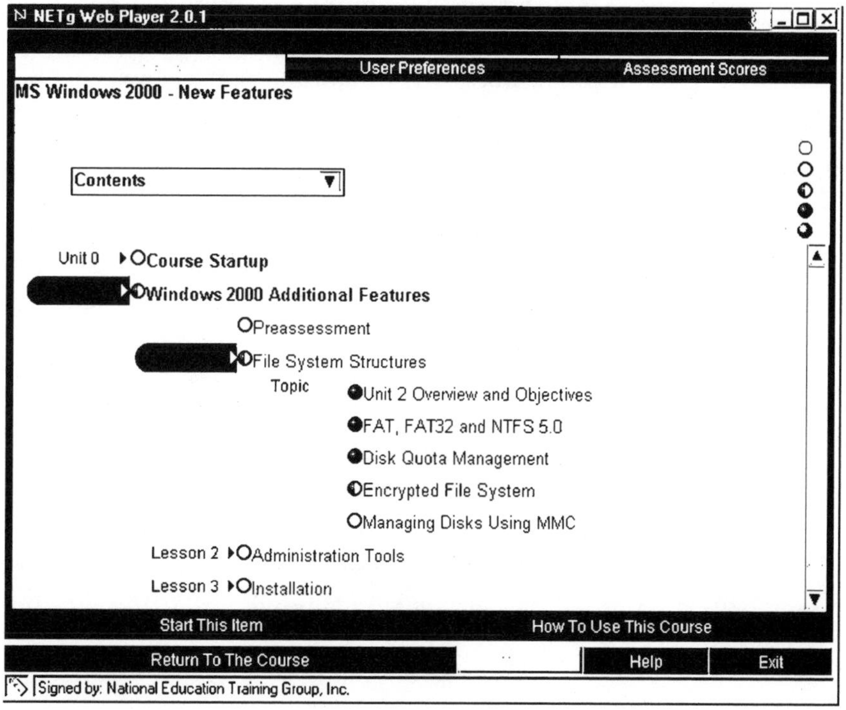

Leader-Led

Leader-led e-learning refers to courses or modules that instructors lead or teach online. Leader-led e-learning is sometimes called instructor–led (ILT). In fact, ILT is a very popular term to describe this type of learning. However, the term leader-led is broader than instructor-led, as it includes instructors, coaches, mentors, and online facilitators. True e-learning exploits this full range of people who facilitate learning, so I prefer the term leader-led e-learning.

In some cases, instructors closely lead the course. In others, the course is largely self-study and the instructor provides assistance as needed. There is a trend toward adding instructors to self-paced courses. They may do this live (synchronously) with video. Leader-led is also delivered in a delayed mode with messages posted to a threaded discussion (asynchronously). The video approach is often used to demonstrate software and for other learning activities where it is important to see a video image. The threaded discussion is excellent for discussing concepts. Figure 1.2 illustrates a threaded discussion from a leader-led course at Royal Roads University.[8] The messages shown are the ones that were used to start a course.

Performance Support Tools

Performance support tools are the last category in our four-type e-learning model. The concept is quite simple: online help for performing some task. When you are operating software, for example, a performance support tool helps you along. Performance support tools are sometimes called electronic performance support tools, electronic performance support systems (EPSS), or wizards.

Figure 1.3 illustrates a performance support tool in MS Word. The dialog box allows you to select a template for different types of documents. Currently, the user has selected Letters & Faxes. When the user clicks on the Envelope Wizard, the Fax Wizard, or the Letter Wizard, interactive instructions appear to coach him or her through preparing an envelope, fax, or letter.[9]

FIGURE 1.2. A WEB SITE ILLUSTRATING LEADER-LED E-LEARNING.

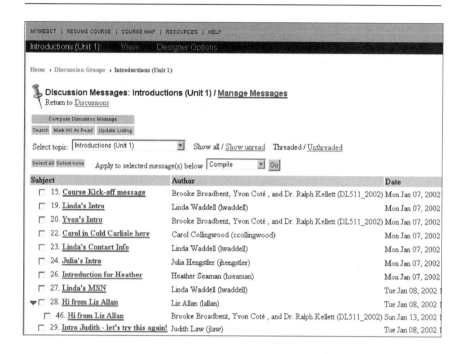

FIGURE 1.3. AN ELECTRONIC PERFORMANCE SUPPORT TOOL IN MS WORD.

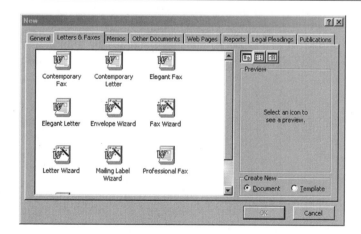

What's in a Name?

A potential purchaser probing a vendor at a trade show:

Shopper: Hi. What are you selling?

Vendor: Async WBT.

Shopper: Is there an instructor?

Vendor: Never. You don't need one with async WBT.
Saves your pennies that way.

Shopper: Then it's self-paced WBT that you sell?

Vendor: Yes. I guess you could call it that. It's available 24/7. Any time.
Anywhere. Guess that is self-paced. You provide the students.
We provide the total solution.

Defining e-learning is a lexicographer's nightmare. The terms cited above are not universally or consistently used. And some are used interchangeably. Informal learning is also known as performance support, informal e-learning, online documentation, multimedia, Web site, hub, or portal, and online learning. Self-paced e-learning is also called self-study, WBT, CBT, multimedia, distance learning, distributed learning, and online learning. Leader-led e-learning is also known as instructor-led learning, ILT, e-ILT, WBT, online distance education, distance learning, distributed learning, and online learning. Performance support tools are sometimes called electronic performance support systems (EPSS), wizards, online help, and online learning—to name a few. There are also IBI, IMI, and CMC. Confused?

Given the diversity in the use of e-learning terminology, it is important to verify what people mean when they use any of these terms. Two people might use the same term to mean very different things. The term online learning, for example, might refer to any of the four types we have outlined here. When someone uses the terms online learning, e-learning, distributed learning, or distance learning, you cannot be certain what they mean. You need to probe.

Choosing Your Route

How can you decide which of the four types of e-learning to use? A simple way to look at it, like most things in life, is to think of your choice of technologies as being influenced by the five W's and their three how friends: who, what, where, when, why, how, how much, and how many. Table 1.2 illustrates the differences among the four types in the way these factors come into play when considering which to use in a particular situation.

Making a Determination

The scheme in Table 1.2 is not as complex as it might seem at first. Certain criteria point instructors, designers, and managers to a particular type of e-learning. For instance, leader-led is often less expensive to develop, and self-study is often best for large groups. You can experience aspects of the e-learning decision-making process first hand by reading the following four scenarios and deciding which type you favor for each. Perhaps any of the four types could be used in each of the four scenarios, and it might even be best to include conventional approaches, too. However, for the purpose of this exercise, choose the *one* type in each case that meets the criteria outlined in Table 1.2.

Case 1: Learning New Software

Two large management consulting corporations have merged. They have different financial and reporting systems. As a result, one has to change its monthly reporting software. Management has opted for e-learning to teach the new software. The target audience is composed of independent learners. They have successfully used a similar suite of software for several years, but there are a few new features they need to learn that are important to the smooth functioning of the corporation. It is anticipated that an instructor will

TABLE 1.2. CRITERIA INFLUENCING THE SELECTION
OF E-LEARNING METHOD.

Criteria	Question	Leader-Led	Informal Learning	Self-Study	Performance Support
Who	is learning?	Somewhat independent learners	Independent learners		
Who	is instructing?	A skilled instructor	No instructor required		
What	is learners' level of knowledge of using computers?	Moderate			High
When	are learners available?	Various times			
Where	do people prefer to learn?	Anywhere, as long as they have a computer and in some cases Internet access			
Why	is the learning necessary?	Lack of ability to discuss, write, think clearly about a topic	Lack of specific knowledge		
How	do learners prefer to learn?	Listening, reading, discussing, doing	Reading	Doing, reading	Doing or watching
How much	time does the organization have to develop e-learning?	Requires instructional materials in days or weeks	Requires instructional materials in weeks or months		
How many	learners?	Excellent for twenty or fewer at a time, but can vary depending on the topic	can handle unlimited numbers of learners		

not be required. In a quick study it was found that the potential learners lack specific knowledge. It was also determined that all members of the group have advanced computer skills. They are mobile workers, stationed in different time zones worldwide; and as a result they work on varying shifts. Their work requires that they have a laptop computer with them at all times. They use these computers to input their monthly travel expenses. As for learning styles, these are hands-on people who prefer to learn by doing. The organization has a reasonable budget for helping some five thousand learners acquire the knowledge they will need to use the new software.

Select one of the four types of e-learning. Would you use informal learning, self-paced, leader-led, or electronic performance support tools?

Case 2: Learning Language Skills

A large financial institution functions in two languages. It is important to have the capacity to serve clients in both languages, as about 20 percent of clients demand service, mostly in written correspondence, in the minority language. Some five hundred employees work in both languages. About two thousand employees work in the majority language only. The main language has tended to predominate over the years, and as a result second-language skills are lagging behind. The institution is looking for an e-learning solution. The target audience is composed of independent learners. The content of the training would be the basic rules of writing the second language. Speaking is not an issue. Learners would be tweaking existing skills. Consequently, it is anticipated that an instructor will not be required. Most members have moderate computer skills, and some have advanced skills. They have busy schedules but they have time for refresher training from time to time. They have computers on their desks. These are hands-on people who prefer to learn by doing. The organization has a substantial budget for helping all employees enhance their linguistic skills.

Which of the four types of e-learning would you select: informal learning, self-paced, leader-led, or electronic performance support tools?

Case 3: Learning New Procedures

A research institute is developing new procedures for critical business processes. All staff will have to learn these new procedures. They are highly educated, independent learners. The information is straightforward and can be learned without an instructor. The learners have general knowledge about the procedures, but there are some new, specific things to learn. All members of the group have moderate computer skills. They have busy schedules and it is difficult to bring them all together at one time. Every office has a desktop computer. As for learning styles, these people, many of whom have doctorates, prefer to learn by reading. The organization has a reasonable budget for helping some two thousand learners acquire the knowledge they will need to use the new procedures.

Select one of the four types of e-learning. Which one will it be?

Case 4: Learning New Management Skills

A public sector organization has been criticized for its management practices. As a result, some two thousand managers have been targeted for training. They are moderately educated, somewhat independent learners. However, their knowledge of management principles and practices is thin. It is a topic they seldom discuss or think about. All members of the group use computers at the moderate level. All potential learners have a desktop computer. They work a regular 9 to 5 day. They have acquired their expertise through stories as well as by trial and error. The employer has a reasonable budget for helping these managers take training to enhance their management skills.

Select one of the four types of e-learning. Which one will it be?

And the Answer Is . . .

Table 1.3 gives "answers" to the four scenarios outlined above. It's not cast in concrete, and in reality organizations often use more than one approach. These are simplified cases. In another situation in which you were teaching new software, language skills, new procedures, or management skills, you might not select the same type of e-learning advocated below, depending on the specific circumstances.

TABLE 1.3. SUGGESTED E-LEARNING APPROACHES FOR CASES.

Case	Type of e-Learning Recommended	Rationale
1. Learning New Software	Performance support	Responds to learners' existing high level of knowledge; the group's advanced computer skills; and the fact that they are spread around the world
2. Learning Language Skills	Self-study	Considers the fact that learners will be tweaking existing skills; the fact that there is time for self-study; and the substantial budget of the organization
3. Learning New Procedures	Informal learning	Fits well with learners' level of education; high degree of independence; and preference to learn by reading
4. Learning New Management Skills	Leader-led, synchronous	Accommodates the small size of the group; their lack of basic knowledge; and their penchant for learning by discussing

The Secret Is in the Blend

Our selection exercise forced you to choose one of the four types of e-learning. Of course, it's never that simple. e-Learning's richness is achieved by combining the four types and also by combining e-learning with conventional learning methods. Firms such as Verizon and IBM have developed performance improvement programs that tap into the four types of e-learning as well as conventional learning.

Here is an overview of programs that Verizon delivers to new recruits and that IBM uses to help seasoned employees who are moving into management ranks. Why combine the four types with conventional learning methods? As you will see below, sometimes formal training is not required. In such cases, informal learning is the best solution. In other situations, workers require a performance support tool to help them perform a task. In other situations, people are capable of working ahead on their own, so self-paced learning is the best solution. Sometimes an online instructor is required to facilitate discussion, debate, and sharing of information. In another situation, it may be best to bring people together in a conventional classroom to ensure that everyone receives the same message.

Verizon's Approach to Training Sales Reps

Verizon trained newly hired sales representatives throughout the United States to sell Internet products and services.[10] They used a "bricks and clicks" approach, starting with a face-to-face mentoring program and then moving to online delivery. The e-learning side involves leader-led e-learning, a knowledge bank (for informal e-learning), individual self-study assignments, and performance support tools.

Table 1.4 shows how Verizon uses the four types of e-learning in combination with conventional learning to train new sales reps.

TABLE 1.4. VERIZON'S MIX OF E-LEARNING
AND CONVENTIONAL LEARNING.

Leader-Led	Informal Learning	Self-Paced	Performance Support	Conventional
Used to teach writing, pre- sentation tech- niques, and selling skills. Leader-led instruction also includes role-playing exercises.	The learners use the Knowl- edge Bank to access product print guides. They can use this infor- mation for homework assignments.	To simulate the real job, home- work assign- ments are created to represent real problems faced by salespeople who sell com- plex Internet products and services. Learners also	Video clips simulate cus- tomer scenarios. This enables learners to work their way through a series of choices. The sales reps make a choice, and the cus- tomer reacts in either a positive	Starts with a mentoring pro- gram allowing learners to meet with experts one-on-one, includes on-site orientation, and links learners up with members of the sales man- agement team who will answer

Leader-Led	**Informal Learning**	**Self-Paced**	**Performance Support**	**Conventional**
		gain valuable role-playing experience in a Web-based training (WBT) environment by practicing sales techniques on a variety of customer personalities and in numerous scenarios.	or negative way. The scenario continues until learners win or lose their sales, based on their choices.	questions throughout the program. By showing learners how everything in the training program relates to the real world, mentoring bring out questions and helps to put the e-learning in the context of the work to be performed.

The IBM Blended Approaches to Learning

IBM uses the four types of e-learning and conventional learning to train new managers. In this "clicks and bricks" approach, participants start with a leader-led online course, proceed to self-study with online simulations and discussion groups, followed six months later by a one-week classroom course. Throughout, informal learning and performance support materials are available. (See Table 1.5 on page 26)

It's Not That Simple

The final decision of which type of e-learning to use in a given situation, or whether to use e-learning at all, will depend on a host of factors. There will most certainly be financial considerations, as well as many contextual considerations. As we explain in subsequent chapters, successful e-learning is developed in the context of the organization, including considerations of what the business need is for the initiative, what the levels of commitment are, and what the preferred instructional methodologies are. Part Two of

TABLE 1.5. IBM'S BLENDED APPROACH TO MANAGEMENT TRAINING.

Leader-Led	Self-Paced	Informal Learning	Performance Support	Conventional
In the first phase, groups of participants take courses over the company intranet. These courses deal with the skills involved in becoming an IBM manager.	The second phase uses simulations to give learners an opportunity to work through business problems, deal with compensation and benefits issues, and build management skills. In the third phase, participants use Lotus Team Room and Lotus Learning Space to solve problems as a group. At any given time, hundreds of small groups will be learning simultaneously.	Throughout, participants have access to commonly asked questions and answers via the Web.	Participants in the first phase have access to a database of scenarios about issues such as handling conflict and retaining employees.	In the second phase, participants receive face-to-face coaching from second-line IBM managers. In the fourth phase, after six months of e-learning, each class meets for one week of classroom activities. They do teamwork activities and use the information they have learned in other phases of the program.

this book covers these issues—and many more—in depth and also provides you with a variety of conceptual frameworks, step-by-step methodologies, and tips and tools to consider for your move toward e-learning. Before getting into the details, however, we will look further into the opportunities and challenges e-learning holds and what we might gain from other organizations who have already learned some lessons in the trenches.

Test Drive

You have been invited to make recommendations on whether your organization should embrace e-learning. People who will be making the decision do not realize that there are four types of e-learning. How would you explain this to them? Prepare the topics you would cover.

Four Types of e-Learning	What Would You Tell People in Your Organization About Each Type?
1.	
2.	
3.	
4.	

CHAPTER TWO

REWARDS AND RISKS

Technological innovations tend to create benefits and pitfalls. Cellular phones are a good example, and so is e-learning. Cell phones put users in touch with kin, clients, and colleagues instantly, but they disrupt work, undermine privacy, and contribute to unsafe driving habits. As for e-learning, on the upside, it can enhance the bottom line by making an organization more productive, saving money, and providing more learners more access to more training. On the downside, e-learning may reduce personal contact between instructors and learners and among the learners themselves—something that many learners highly value. High dropout rates are a warning of this potential pitfalls of e-learning. e-Learning managers, developers, and instructors face the double-barrel challenge of maximizing the benefits of e-learning and minimizing its downside. In this chapter we will review both sides and suggest some ways to avoid e-learning's pitfalls and reap its rewards.

Putting Yourself into the Driver's Seat

The central focus of e-learning, as for traditional learning, is *learning*. Therefore it is not surprising that a discussion about the challenges and opportunities in e-learning is equally applicable to traditional learning methods.

Some of the issues in both traditional learning and e-learning are (1) relevant content focused on business issues, (2) clear explanations of content, and (3) application of content to real-world experience. On the delivery side, learning occurs best when an instructional strategy includes individualized learning, nurturing, questioning, and frequent interaction with learners, leaders, and content.

Read the following from Allison Rossett on why she dropped out of an e-learning class.

> "I wish I could point to the class and blame them for turning me off. I can't. The things that made me drop out are the same things that make the Web so compelling. The beauty of 'anywhere, any time, whenever you want' too readily turns into not now, maybe later, and often not at all. Lacking a dynamic instructor, powerful incentives, links to the job, and fixed schedules, Web learning is at a dramatic disadvantage in capturing and holding attention. In my pajamas, near computer, phone, refrigerator, cats, and pals, it was just too easy to do everything except my Web class."[1]   —Allison Rossett is a professor of educational
> technology at San Diego State University and the author
> of *Beyond the Podium: Delivering Training and Performance to a Digital World* and *First Things Fast: A Handbook for Performance Analysis.*

Generally, e-learners appreciate the convenience, choice, and flexibility that e-learning offers. Instructional designers value the standardized framework and flexibility of e-learning media. Instructors think e-learning is convenient; they applaud the ease of record keeping and the reduced travel that are part of the e-learning revolution. Managers like the idea of automated, consistent assessment information and the reduced costs that e-learning can bring to an organization. Let's try to understand these different perspectives now. Being able to see how key e-learning stakeholders view it can help us grasp e-learning better.

The Learner's Perspective

> "When I study online, there is no sitting in the back of the class. The instructor forces us to participate. It is more work than other courses. But I learn more."   —George, an e-learning student

George is not alone. What he experienced in a college many others are experiencing in the corporate world. For example, some three hundred sales representatives of a nationwide communications corporation recently had a positive e-learning experience—or at least a majority of them did.

When their company launched an innovative technology, the sales reps learned about the features of the new device through an e-learning program. In addition to online modules, the reps could access a threaded discussion where they posted questions and received answers from experts, any time, any place (if they had the required technology). The sales reps appreciated the fact that they did not have to spend long hours flying to headquarters for training. Instead they could go to their regional offices across the country. Also, when they were traveling they used hotel telephone lines to connect to the corporation's servers to obtain the latest technical information and to check the postings to the threaded discussion. As a result of the time saved, they had additional time to make calls, sell the new product—and meet their sales targets.

The reps who gained the most out of this program were the most self-motivated ones. They carefully arranged their schedules to take the training. They were curious and made full use of the hyperlinks in the e-learning materials that led to sites on the World Wide Web. The less motivated learners longed for the classroom, where this type of instruction had been conducted in the past. They missed the camaraderie of fellow reps from across the country, the war stories, and the opportunity to spend a few days at an upscale hotel.

Ten Benefits for Learners. What are some of the much-talked-about benefits of e-learning? Here are ten attributes of well-designed e-learning. From the point of view of learners, well-designed e-learning:

1. Creates interactions that stimulate understanding and the recall of information when learners exchange questions during online discussions.
2. Accommodates different types of learners and fosters learning through a variety of activities that apply different learning styles.
3. Fosters self-paced learning so learners can learn at the rate they prefer.
4. Provides convenient access to learning any time, any place.
5. Reduces travel time and travel costs.

6. Encourages learners to browse for information through hyperlinks to sites on the World Wide Web.
7. Allows learners to select targeted and appropriate material on the Web.
8. Provides context-sensitive help through performance support tools.
9. Develops technical abilities required to use the Internet.
10. Encourages learners to take responsibility for their learning and builds self-knowledge and self-confidence.

Notice I did not say these are the strong points of *all* e-learning. Successful, engaging e-learning, like scrumptious food, is the product of high-quality ingredients, tender loving care, and craftsmanship. In other words, opening up the cake mix box of e-learning ingredients does not produce instant results. Best results are achieved when you work carefully with the prepackaged materials. Add essential ingredients. Mix. Bake to perfection. And serve on an attractive dish.

The Instructor's Perspective

> "I like the fact that I don't need to commute to headquarters to conduct our e-learning programs. That way I can devote more time to participants and work with them on real-life applications."
>
> —Charles, a corporate e-learning leader

Charles leads a double existence as a professor of business management for a New York college and an instructor for an international pharmaceutical manufacturing firm. Normally, he teaches in a leader-led mode in the classroom; however, he seized the opportunity to instruct online when both his college and company extended the offer. Charles uses the resources of the World Wide Web to insert international examples into his courses. By offering courses in a Web-based format, Charles provides individualized online coaching to learners through email. At the same time, he posts these individual email coaching notes to a threaded discussion group so that all participants can read his advice. He is able to do all this work from his home office, thereby avoiding several hours of tedious commuting. Although he is separated from the e-learners by many miles and he never meets them face to face, Charles finds that he strikes up relationships that continue after the course.

Seven Benefits of e-Learning for Instructors. From the perspective of instructors, the benefits of e-learning include:

1. Provides convenient access for instructors any time, any place.
2. Allows pre-packaging of essential information for all students to access and frees instructors to concentrate on high-level activities in the delivery phase.
3. Retains records of discussion and allows for later reference through the use of a threaded discussion or streaming video.
4. Generates more personal gratification for instructors through quality e-learner participation.
5. Reduces travel and accommodation costs associated with training programs.
6. Encourages instructors to access up-to-date resources on the Web.
7. Allows instructors to communicate information in a more engaging fashion than possible in text-based distance education programs.

The Online Developer's Perspective

> "When I create an online course, all the course information is in one place. I don't need to worry about making handouts for various classes. It is all on our intranet, for learners to access, any time, anywhere."
> —Tracy, e-learning course developer

Tracy has developed leader-led training materials for more than twenty years. When the opportunity came to convert three existing leader-led courses to an asynchronous, instructor-facilitated e-learning format, Tracy asked for and was given the assignment. Once the format was set for one course, Tracy was able to use it for the other two. In fact, there were some elements in each course that Tracy was able to use in the other courses. The Web-based training was facilitated by the use of existing Web-based resources. Tracy included a threaded discussion and found that students entered into meaningful discussion. All discussion was recorded for later review.

Eight Benefits for Online Developers. Developers who have had success with e-learning have found that it:

1. Promotes the orderly layout of course materials, assignments, and general administration through a Web site.
2. Sets a framework for rapidly updating learning materials.
3. Encourages the use of innovative, interactive tools such as polls and quizzes.
4. Facilitates the linking of learning to tools for competency assessment and performance management.
5. Facilitates access to a rich assortment of existing Web-based resources.
6. Allows for automated replies to knowledge-based questions.
7. Fosters meaningful exchanges among participants through the discussion capabilities of the Internet.
8. Adds an engaging, personalized element through technologies such as audio files and streaming video and personalized videoconferencing equipment.

The Manager's Perspective

> "We have instructors retiring in the next few years. Capturing their expertise in an online learning program will help to ensure that we don't lose their expertise."   —William, a training manager

An international consulting firm had a tradition of holding five-day orientation sessions for new hires at expensive locations worldwide. Combining pre-session e-learning with a shortened two-day orientation course, the company was able to reduce the length of the orientation session, provide the program to larger groups, and deliver it much sooner after they were hired. Equally if not more important, the company was able to make substantial savings, engender consistency, and expose a larger number of new hires to their best instructors. With e-learning, managers were able to assess the knowledge and track the progress of new hires and organize them into similar groups for the two-day, face-to-face, team-building component of their training.

Seven Benefits for Managers. Managers who have had success with e-learning comment that it can:

1. Provide automated, continuous assessment and reporting of student participation and progress.
2. Reduce capital costs associated with traditional brick-and-mortar schools and training facilities.
3. Reduce costs of learning materials, mailing, and telephones associated with distance learning programs.
4. Allow access to the same materials through a variety of platforms such as Windows, UNIX, and Mac through the use of html files in a browser.
5. Create more consistency in the training program through a template approach.
6. Create a one-stop shopping center through training coordination software to offer courses from across the organization.
7. Provide access to leading instructors worldwide.

How to Fail

Throughout this book we concentrate on how to *succeed* with e-learning. Why talk about failure now? It's simple. There are many pitfalls awaiting anyone becoming involved in e-learning. You may recognize the thoughts and actions in our tongue-in-cheek dos and don'ts lists here; perhaps you have experienced them first hand. They are prevalent behaviors, and once you see them for what they are, you will be in a position to do something about them.

Dos and Don'ts for e-Learner Failure

- Don't ask for help
- Expect e-learning to be the same as conventional learning
- Fit e-learning study time in whenever you can
- Expect instructors to provide everything you need
- Lurk and never participate

Dos and Don'ts for e-Learning Leader Failure

- Do not set a structure for the course
- Turn the learners loose on new technology and software without any preparation
- When learners have problems with technology, refer them to the help desk and accept no responsibility for assisting students with technology problems
- Present an online lecture the same way you would a classroom lecture
- Do not use Web resources from other sites
- Use the same group facilitation skills online that you use in person

Dos and Don'ts for e-Learning Developer Failure

- Do not consult with stakeholders when developing learning materials
- Concentrate on content, not on learning
- Use the latest technology and plug-ins to create pizzazz, whether relevant or not
- Do not conduct alpha and beta testing to tweak training materials
- Design one-size-fits-all e-learning materials
- Be a purist; never combine e-learning with conventional learning approaches

Dos and Don'ts for e-Learning Manager Failure

- Expect e-learning to sell itself without a communication plan
- Keep your plans, issues, and progress to yourself
- Insist on off-the-shelf solutions exclusively
- Designate one of the four types of e-learning as a silver bullet
- Don't plan an evaluation

> "When I started to develop e-learning, I had no help. So it was difficult at first. I wish I had taken the time to learn about all the resources that exist."
> —Allan, e-learning course leader

Taking a Wrong Turn: A Lesson from a Client

Many things can go wrong when e-learning is poorly designed and executed. One example is the following story from one of our clients.

In the past, officers in a large metropolitan police force had followed a structured program in which management made most of the training decisions. When the organization implemented e-learning, it took a hands-off approach. Officers selected which courses to take and when to take them. No efforts were made to add technical support or to orient the officers to the new technology. The underlying assumption was that people would be motivated to learn to use e-learning on their own.

After a few months, it was apparent that some officers lagged behind in selecting and completing their courses. In some cases the program blended e-learning with classroom studies, with the e-learning module designed to be completed before the classroom section. A few learners completed the e-learning component, but many did not. This placed the classroom instructor in the difficult position of having to decide whether to present the course as if everyone had completed the e-learning segment or to cover all the information from the e-learning segment in the classroom course, thereby catering to students who had not completed the e-learning segment.

Training management staff surveyed several officers to determine why they had not taken the e-learning instruction. To their surprise, they learned that some of the officers did not have access to the required hardware. Some were trying to use CBT with voice and music on computers that lacked sound cards. These officers had not realized what the problem was; they just assumed that the e-learning materials, in this case CBT on a CD-ROM, did not work properly. A few had the technology but did not know how to use it. And some had tried to get help from the technical support group—to no avail, because the help desk was swamped by calls. There were also other learners who were simply resisting anything to do with computers and e-learning.

The program was deemed a fiasco, and it led the organization to revisit its thinking about e-learning. Eventually the organization succeeded with e-learning, even though the initial failure generated negative, long-lasting consequences. The second time around, training leaders consulted extensively with all affected parties, including the information technology group, management, instructors, and members of the target group. The roll-out included orientation sessions, extensive technical support, and individual help for resistors. The leaders of the e-learning initiative now saw themselves as agents of change and they planned carefully how to deal with challenges. They selected champions and followed a careful change management program.

Meeting the Challenges

Other organizations have faced similar challenges. If you ask a few users about their experience with e-learning, you'll likely hear a long litany of difficult problems. Don't be surprised if users tell you about technical glitches. Some will regret the lack of face-to-face contact. Many will probably tell you that the content and design of e-learning needs to be better thought out. Many self-paced e-learning programs remain electronic page turners, with more text than learners can cope with. Many leader-led sessions lack vitality, engagement, and clever tactics to engage learners.

Eleven Common Challenges and Responses

At the same time, there are success stories galore. This is not to say that successful e-learning programs were conceived and implemented without a hitch. Many organizations failed with their first attempts at e-learning. They identified reasons for failure, regrouped, redesigned, and eventually succeeded. A challenge waits at every decision point, but forewarned is forearmed and every challenge can be responded to effectively. Table 2.1 outlines some of the hurdles you might face in implementing e-learning and some responses that have worked in other organizations.

TABLE 2.1. E-LEARNING CHALLENGES AND RESPONSES.

Challenge	Response
1. e-Learning represents a new way of addressing learning.	Learners, instructors, developers, and managers need to plan their training and follow their plan. A formative evaluation involving focus groups as the course progresses is a good way to assess whether these plans are working. Ongoing evaluation also keeps everyone tuned to developments and helps to identify areas for change as the training progresses.
2. Learners require new computer equipment.	Organizations can either provide the new equipment or financially assist learners to acquire it. Training equipment budgets should include funds to teach students how to use the new equipment.

Challenge	**Response**
3. Learners and instructors are hampered by technical difficulties, including operator error.	Provide a help desk seven days a week, twenty-four hours a day. Train the help desk people well. Ensure that the help desk staff have first-hand experience with the issues.
4. Students and instructors have gaps in their computer knowledge.	Identify what knowledge is required. Assess individuals against the standard. Identify individual gaps. Provide training to bridge the gaps. Appoint and train coaches to help after training or in lieu of formal training. Reward coaches. Set entry qualifications and ensure that students meet the qualifications.
5. Instructors and designers may not have experience with e-learning.	Provide the opportunity for instructors and designers to participate in a course that teaches how to facilitate and develop e-learning.
6. Development costs are high, depending on the training approach taken.	Start with low-end approaches. You might, for example, start with a blended approach with two days in the classroom and thirty hours of online instruction.
7. Plug-ins are difficult to load, especially for novices.	Avoid plug-ins or, if absolutely necessary, go with well-supported ones and provide solid help with loading them.
8. Bandwidth and hardware may not support the use of multimedia or video over the Internet.	Be cautious when introducing multimedia or video to e-learning. Look for the lower tech solution. For example, instead of synchronous online video, use slides and voice-over.
9. Implementing e-learning is complex. There are many stakeholders. They have different points of view.	Consult key players. Identify their concerns. Address them. Stakeholders include employees, instructors, developers, management, and the information technology group.
10. In some organizations, management and staff launch e-learning without a solid understanding of what they are tackling and they are not mentally prepared to make the commitment that is required to reap the benefits.	Include an extensive communications program with the introduction of e-learning. Identify distinct target groups. Tell each group what the implications of e-learning are for them. Add a personal touch to the implementation by crafting stories about the people who are associated with e-learning implementation. Keep the stories upbeat. Deliver your message through various media (email, a Web site, person to person, and posters).

Challenge	Response
11. Resisters hide their heads in the sand and pretend that e-learning does not exist.	You may not be able to get everyone on board, but you can increase your number of supporters by finding champions at middle and senior levels who establish the expectation that e-learning will be used. These champions have also been used to personally congratulate learners after they have completed a significant block of studies.

As e-learning evolves, challenges ranging from lack of equipment or computer literacy to deep-seated organizational resistance are being faced and resolved. However, there will always be new challenges. To meet them, learners, instructors, developers, and managers need the following characteristics:

- A realistic understanding of the strengths and weaknesses of e-learning
- Full commitment to making e-learning work successfully
- Flexibility, creativity, and the diligence required to adapt e-learning to the specific needs of individuals and organizations
- The conviction to say no when they think e-learning is not the right solution to a business performance issue

The case of the Microsoft Certified Systems Engineer (MCSE) course below illustrates how one organization learned from some of the inherent problems. Resolving the issues illustrated here took sound judgment and patience.

Case 1: Certification Woes

To prepare for the MCSE examination, participants in an online program studied for thirty-one weeks part-time. Their ages covered the spectrum from twenties to fifties. They were all employed full-time. Most were married. Several had young children. Approximately half were women. None had the funds nor the support system to take the program full-time. All were taking the program to improve their career prospects.

The only scheduled time with the instructor was a lecture between 7 and 9 p.m. on Tuesday and Thursday, every week for thirty-one weeks. The instructor used NetMeeting to demonstrate what he was teaching. None of the NetMeeting materials were saved for later review by learners. He was also available for ad hoc discussion using chat software. All students could log on to the instant message service (ICQ) and participate in the same discussion. The discussions in ICQ were archived for later reference.

In a focus group meeting (with spouses over a meal), participants told us of benefits, technical challenges, their exhaustion, and lessons learned.

Benefits

As might be expected, the learners were enthusiastic about the schedule of this course: outside of their normal workday and only four hours a week. The scheduling of the virtual classes allowed them to keep their full-time jobs and do their self-study whenever they could find a block of time. Participants saved considerable time by being able to simply go to their computers, rather than driving to the college offering the program. They found that the instructor was able to explain things clearly with NetMeeting. A number also commented that they felt the "free" computer that came with the course was terrific. Students also thought the instructor went to great lengths to be available for chatting with them over ICQ.

Technical Challenges

When asked in our focus group what the participants would change, one quickly retorted, "A system that did not crash." Nervous laughter and head nodding from fellow students—and spouses—followed this statement!

Although NetMeeting worked well technically, there were some glitches. For example, the instructor would use terms that he assumed the participants knew, such as "applet" and "IE." Participants felt that in a normal classroom situation an instructor would see the confused looks on their faces and explain some of these terms. Even when they did ask questions about terminology, in a dynamic chat session some questions were not answered. It seems that the instructor did not review the chat session notes after the class and, consequently, often left questions unanswered.

Also, in a normal classroom, participants would have been able to see computer parts, hold them, and generally get first-hand knowledge of the physical set-up. One participant commented that it was not until he saw a basic computer part in an electronics shop that he knew what the piece was that the online instructor had referred to and understood how to use it.

Physical and Mental Exhaustion

The e-learners and their spouses said that they were exhausted from the experience. One spouse said he had lost twenty-five pounds during the program. Another participant commented that he no longer had time to visit the gym so he put on ten pounds. The long hours dedicated to self-study prevented the learners from taking holidays, and young mothers felt they had been "tested" by their kids. One mother of two pre-school-age girls normally put her children to bed between seven and nine—when the online lecture was given. They refused to let their Dad put them to bed and, as a result, Mom had to leave her computer to do it. Normally the bedtime ritual took ten minutes; now it sometimes took an hour.

Would They Do It Again?

When asked whether they wished to repeat the experience, several commented that, in taking one course, they had developed the skills required to function effectively in any online learning environment. Some said, however, that if they had known how difficult it was going to be, they would not have started the course. When participants came together at the end of the program to discuss their experiences, they said they wished they had met earlier, identified problems, and developed solutions.

Lessons Learned

Here are some lessons for e-learners, designers, instructors, and managers that can be taken from the Microsoft Certification example. Do you see others?

1. *Time Required:* Designers should take into account the real-life needs of the target learners. In the case of the MCSE program, course learners had three commitments for thirty-one weeks—one to their jobs, one to the MCSE course, the third to their families. Some found it difficult to squeeze their families into that schedule. No wonder some of the participants said they would not repeat the experience.
2. *Computer Literacy:* The instructor made false assumptions about participants' knowledge of basic computer technology and terminology. Instructors need to create an environment in which students feel at ease asking basic questions.

3. *Equipment:* Every effort needs to be taken to ensure that the computer system used to deliver e-learning is up to the task. Technology glitches must be reduced to a minimum.

4. *Participant Expectations:* Participants need to be realistic in their commitments. It is extremely challenging to complete a comprehensive e-learning program, hold down a job, and help raise a family at the same time.

5. *Scheduling:* The lecture at a specified time approach did not accommodate some members of the group. Streamed video would have been more effective—allowing a synchronous (any time) viewing.

Keeping Things in Context

When trying to assess the lessons learned from the Microsoft Certification course, keep in mind that this program used scheduled classes, detailed lectures, and chat. Some e-learning programs have none of these elements. Also bear in mind that the MCSE program is a comprehensive, content-rich course of study and that it is followed by a demanding exam. This MCSE course might be an extreme case, but it does serve to warn of some of the pitfalls of online learning—especially the way many organizations put sessions online much as they would be conducted in a classroom.

Three Parting Tips

We have placed e-learning under a magnifying glass in this chapter. Magnification allows us to understand essential qualities. At the same time, a magnifying glass tends to distort reality. We have exaggerated the challenges with e-learning in the sense that listing them together suggests they all would occur in any one e-learning intervention. That is not the case. By focusing on the issues associated with e-learning, we could be giving the impression that e-learning is radically different from anything that preceded it. Again, that's not the case.

The technology of e-learning may be new, but its underlying approach to solving problems is the same as for conventional learning. Therefore the challenges you face with e-learning must be met with the same coping strategies you have developed for meeting other issues, whether they be in a training context or not.

Here are four general tips for dealing with e-learning challenges that you no doubt already use in other circumstances:

- Look at challenges as opportunities to learn by using a reasoned, problem-solving approach.
- Spend time analyzing the challenge before throwing a solution at it.
- Consult with others who have implemented e-learning because there are probably people and organizations that have faced similar issues to those you will face.
- Thoroughly consult with affected parties. You will be pleasantly surprised by the quality of solutions learners, instructors, developers, and managers will offer. They often have very clear ideas of where enhancements could be made and how to make them.

Test Drive

You have been invited to contribute to a study of e-learning in your organization. You can decide whether the study will concentrate on how to introduce e-learning successfully or on how to improve the current approach to e-learning. We invite you to plan the input you will give to an interviewer. What subjects would you cover? What would you say? Consider the upside and the downside of e-learning.

CHAPTER THREE

LESSONS FROM THE TRENCHES*

Implementing e-learning across an organization is no easy task. First, you need to determine whether or not e-learning is suited to your organization, and then you need to build the "culture" to accommodate it. As with any new endeavor, we can learn much from the experience of others—both positive and negative.

This chapter describes some e-learning successes and failures and suggests what lessons can be drawn from them to help ensure that e-learning is a success in your organization. Each case has been selected to represent a specific element of the e-learning process, from assessing organizational readiness through delivery and evaluation. In each case, we will summarize the organization's experience and then highlight a few key themes that you should keep in mind as you begin to build your own e-learning solution.

As you read each example, think about how it reflects your organization. Do the same issues exist in your company or institution? Are the solutions acceptable? Can you avoid the same mistakes? If so, how? At the end of the chapter, you will find a summary of all the lessons learned from the case studies. You can use this information to build your own checklist of issues to address during e-learning implementation. Many of the themes presented in the examples will be addressed in the remaining chapters of the book.

*Co-author of this chapter was Regan Legassie, training development officer at the Canadian Forces Training Development Centre in CFB Borden, Ontario.

Military Training

Let's start with probably the most ambitious and diverse e-learning effort
we know—providing learning on demand to the men and women of the
Armed Forces of the United States. In particular, the U.S. Army is strug-
gling with the new realities of the digital battlefield:

> As the U.S. Army struggles to move its forces into the 21st Century, it will be-
> come increasingly dependent on soldiers who understand information age
> technologies, are well-versed in the use of digital skills, and can use their
> weapons and equipment to accomplish assigned missions. . . . Recommenda-
> tions can be made to improve training, but more must be done to achieve the
> Army's vision. Distributed learning, embedded training, and Web-delivered
> training hold promise as delivery mechanisms.[1]

Think back to the Persian Gulf War and remember the television footage
of "smart bombs," laser guided missiles, and Patriot Missile systems. All of
these are highly digitized battle systems and require well-trained operators to
be used effectively.[2] Add to this the fact that U.S. Army troops are spread
around the continent (and the world) and e-learning seems to address the
concerns raised above.

Lifelong Learning in the U.S. Army

In 1997, the U.S. Department of Defense (DoD) launched the Advanced Distributed Learning (ADL) initiative to develop common standards for the "look
and feel" of e-learning across the U.S. military. Almost immediately, e-learning
activities began. One of the first was the development of an e-learning network in Iowa to serve the needs of the National Guard.[3] Built primarily around
videoconferencing, the Iowa experiment proved that e-learning could be
used effectively in military training.
   More recently, the U.S. Army implemented a force-wide e-learning
network to serve the educational needs of its people. Through a partnership
with PricewaterhouseCoopers, independent courseware developers, and

universities, the Army initiated goArmy.com in early 2001.[4] Its mandate is to ensure that all members of the Army have access to the education they need to upgrade their skills and knowledge in today's fast-paced world. The e-learning program serves two purposes:

- First, it allows Army personnel to upgrade their education during their careers while still maintaining an active duty role. Soldiers who want a degree but were previously unable to attend a university or college due to deployments or isolated postings can now do so via a computer and the Internet.
- Second, by making learning easy to obtain, the Army hopes to create a force of lifelong learners who are able to adapt and comprehend the tremendous changes technology is having on the face of warfare.

Army Intranet: Larger than the Library of Congress

In yet another example of the military following the e-learning road, in November of 2001, the U.S. Army unveiled its Army Knowledge Online Portal. It allows all active and retired personnel to access hundreds of Army internal sites, servers, and resources. Three times larger than the storage capacity of the Library of Congress, the network will provide access for the estimated one million to three million users. Information will be personalized and targeted, based on a person's rank, experience, location, and duties.[5]

As a side note, the Army hopes that its large-scale use of e-learning will also serve as an incentive to recruiting. Increasingly, employees are listing opportunities for education and self-development as a high priority, so the Army is hoping its initiative will accommodate this desire.

Military Recruiting and Specialist Training Britain

The military in the United Kingdom is also looking to e-learning as a solution to its recruiting and education requirements. In its recent review of defense policy, the U.K. Ministry of Defense (MOD) noted that two key trends were leading the push toward e-learning: shifting social trends and increases in technology.[6] Today, the average military recruit in Britain has a higher level of education than in past years—between 60 and 90 percent of recruits come in with some post-secondary education and a desire to keep learning throughout their careers. The increasing complexity of military technology and recent advances in telecommunications (the second reason outlined in the study) strengthened the case for implementing e-learning, so much so that the U.K. Ministry of Defense has decreed that "80 percent of appropriate classroom-based specialist training courses [will] incorporate a minimum of 25 percent e-learning within five years [2003]."[7]

This will not be an easy task, and four requirements have been identified for implementation to be effective:

1. A communications infrastructure that will allow e-learning delivery must be established. It would serve as the clearinghouse for e-learning courses and materials and ensure consistency of design and delivery. Therefore, as the U.K. begins to modernize and amalgamate its existing communications infrastructure, it has pledged to make e-learning a central requirement of this upgrade.
2. Once the e-learning infrastructure is developed, it must be managed with an eye toward the effective overall operation of the program.
3. Facilities and courseware must be developed to put on the network. This will be accomplished through the combination of existing facilities, new purpose built e-learning facilities,[8] rental/lease of civilian facilities, and partnerships with civilian courseware developers.
4. Finally, and perhaps most difficult of all, the U.K. military must educate its own staff that e-learning is just as demanding and just as effective as traditional learning.

The e-learning initiative will be expensive (most of the costs will be in infrastructure and courseware development) but, when combined with other modernization issues, it should save the Ministry of Defense about $1.8 billion over twenty-five years—proof that e-learning is a sound investment.

Medicine

The medical field has also been quick to adopt the benefits of new technologies to help ensure doctors are current on the rapidly changing field of medicine.

Telemedicine in Space

When John Glenn returned to space at the age of 77, his accomplishment seemed astonishing. For NASA, however, there was another problem—how to treat a senior citizen who has a medical emergency a million miles from the nearest hospital with no doctor around? Since you can't keep another shuttle on stand by (that only works in the movies), NASA turned to the next best option—telemedicine.

Telemedicine has been around for a number of years. Originally envisioned as a process of keeping doctors around the country informed using conference calls, videotapes, and closed circuit broadcasts, it has evolved into a serious industry using the conferencing capabilities of the Internet. In the case of John Glenn, NASA went as far as to develop a system that would allow surgeons on earth to perform virtual operations in space.[9] Thankfully, the technology wasn't needed, but it did prove the value of e-learning and technology to medical educators.

Digital CME

Like many professionals, doctors are required to take periodic courses and seminars to upgrade and maintain their skills. Called Continuing Medical Education (CME), this usually requires doctors to book time off from a busy patient load to attend courses at universities or research institutes. The Internet has begun to change all of that.

A number of private corporations have begun to develop and distribute CME via the Internet. The format of these sessions ranges from pre-packaged lectures and presentations to real-time interactive seminars or demonstrations. Advances in bandwidth offer even more potential. The future of this industry is so great that some analysts predict that the Internet could eventually handle 50 percent of all CME. Here's an example of how it works:

"The topic for the evening is advances in suturing techniques. At a pre-arranged time, course participants log on to the Internet and begin to receive a video stream from the ACME School of Medicine. The instructor is a medical professor who will demonstrate the techniques as she explains them to students during a webcast. By clicking on an icon in the screen interface, students are able to ask questions of the instructor and interact with other students to share common experiences or to ask questions. The session is digitally recorded and placed on a server for review at any time by the students or by any other doctor who couldn't attend the webcast. Those who view the "taped" version can email their questions directly to the instructor or designated tutor, who responds to their questions within forty-eight hours."

Sound far-fetched? It isn't. This is actually occurring in several medical schools across the United States. Recent advances in bandwidth have made synchronous webcasts more feasible and appealing; the number of doctors using the Internet continues to increase; and the savings in time has led to an increase in the number of CME events offered via e-learning. For a good example of how this can be done, look at the University of Virginia's e-learning offering called mypatient.com. Using "virtual" patients, students are able to interview, diagnose, treat, and see the effects of various treatments on the patient—a good application of CME via e-learning.

Virtual Surgery

Many medical schools also are making use of new technology to improve classroom training. For example, students at the University of Wisconsin are using complex simulators to learn surgical procedures.[10] If you have ever taken first aid or CPR training, you no doubt have practiced your skills on the Rescue Annie training aid. As you practiced your mouth-to-mouth or CPR techniques, the doll responded as a human subject would.

At Wisconsin, this has been taken one step further. In the surgical classes at the university, the "patient" is programmed with various conditions (ruptured spleen, gunshot wound to the chest, and so forth) and the students are asked to perform surgery to correct the problem. As they operate, the simulator presents them with a steady flow of information such as blood pressure, heart rate, and respiration. Each time they do something, the patient responds accordingly. Occasionally, to demonstrate what can happen in surgery, the instructor will program an emergency into the machine (such as cardiac arrest) and the student will have to react to the situation and "save" the patient.

All of this provides a very realistic environment, yet affords the student an opportunity to make mistakes and learn from them (a key component of adult learning) without endangering the safety of a real patient in the operating room. Currently, the cost of such a system is prohibitively high, but as technology improves and the value of this technology is proven, there's a good chance that the next time you have surgery, your doctor may have learned to perform the operation on a "virtual" patient or at least will have modified the procedure virtually, combined with "hands-on" experience.

Law and B-Schools

Did you know that it is now possible to earn your law degree without ever attending a single class or mock trial? Concord University School of Law has been offering an accredited law degree via e-learning since 1988.[11] Using a combination of synchronous and asynchronous tools, Concord has been able to replicate the law school experience we all remember from watching reruns of John Houseman in "The Paper Chase" television show.

Case Work Online

Like students in a traditional law school, the virtual students at Concord are assigned various cases and case summaries to read and review. Then, instead of discussing them during a face-to-face meeting, students log on to the Concord site and respond to questions posted by the professor and other students. Periodically, the students and the professor will "meet" through the use of computer conferencing. During these synchronous sessions, students can pose questions to the professor via audio or text. The questions and responses are relayed to the rest of the class for information and discussion. Videotaped lectures by visiting faculty and online assignments and quizzes round out the curriculum at Concord.

The challenge in building an online law school was in determining how to make the e-learning format suit the topic. Course developers went back to the basics of a legal education—debate and analysis of case law. Rather than posting a bunch of text online, developers opted to use traditional law books and generate the critical thinking skills via the e-learning technologies.

The advantages of an online law school are considerable.

- First, since most law schools are in large urban areas and require residency, a degree delivered via e-learning opens the door to many students who were previously unable to attend a law school due to job, family, or location commitments.
- Second, time is no longer an issue. Aside from the regularly scheduled synchronous conferences, students are free to work on their courses when they are able—evenings, weekends, early mornings. As long as they complete the course requirements, there is no need to be "in class" at a prescheduled time.
- The third benefit is the student monitoring component of the Concord program—a feature many traditional law schools could probably benefit from. Using the features built into the school's learning management system (LMS), faculty are able to monitor when a student logs in, for how long, and where he or she is in the courseware. This feature allows professors to diagnose which students may be in trouble early in a course, to contact them, and to resolve the problem or provide remedial work to address the shortfalls. The results of this process are impressive. Concord boasts a 73 percent retention rate overall and a 60 to 65 percent rate among first-year students—who traditionally have the highest dropout rates in a conventional law school.

Virtual MBAs

Not to be outdone by the doctors and lawyers, business schools are embracing e-learning as well.

Online at Athabaska

At Athabaska University in Alberta, Canada, students can earn a traditional online MBA or specialize in information technology, agriculture, or project management.[12] When a student registers in the program, he or she is issued the University's LMS—a specially designed computer program that tracks and identifies student coursework and discussion contributions—based on a Lotus Notes® platform.

The students are assigned to teams and issued a case study to resolve or analyze. They are given a problem sequence and instructed to develop a solution for posting by a predetermined deadline. Using email, computer conferencing, and telephones, students work together on the case and post their notes in a review area accessible by the instructor/tutor as they begin to build the response. Once the response is completed, it is "released" to the remainder of the program for discussion and analysis. This cycle is repeated throughout the program.

Athabaska measured the success of its program against a traditional program offered at the Ivey School of Business at the University of Western Ontario in Canada. The results were promising.[13] Athabaska's evaluation compared a face-to-face class of MBA students against an online class. Students were asked to rate the value of each medium for social, procedural, explanatory, and cognitive learning abilities. The reflective nature of e-learning—the ability to read a posting, think about it, and then respond—was a key benefit for the online group. In contrast, the face-to-face group found it easier to develop social connections and leadership, although the difference between the two media was minimal in this category—indicating that the same skills can occur online, but it takes a little while longer to develop them.

With the introduction of online learning, the number of students taking distance education courses at Athabasca University doubled in three years. More importantly, other universities now view Athabasca[14] in a different light. Once considered a fringe institution, Athabasca University now has some 25 percent of the Canadian e-learning MBA market.

Business and Industry

Many business organizations have found e-learning a useful tool to improve productivity and reduce cost. One of these is the Ford Motor Company.

20,000 Engineers e-Learning at Ford

In 1997, the Ford Design Institute was told it had to get twenty thousand engineers through 160 hours of training in four years.[15] Staff at the Institute quickly realized that this could not happen due to scheduling limitations, job functions, and lack of resources. Furthermore, many of the firm's engineering staff viewed the conventional classroom training as redundant or uninteresting. e-Learning was viewed as a solution to the problem.

The design team developed a detailed list of training requirements for e-learning proposals, which they submitted to a list of previously identified suppliers. The magnitude of the problem was quickly apparent to the successful contractor, who then had to "find" the necessary subcontractors to meet the technical and learning requirements of the e-learning program. In the end, the process worked, but not without a few growing pains along the way.

Verizon's Virtual University Trains a Sales Force

Verizon faced the challenging task of training four hundred newly hired sales representatives across the continent to sell complex Internet products and services. The solution was what the company calls an Integrated Learning Solution—now an ongoing combination of instructors, self-paced training on the Web or CD-ROMs, knowledge management systems, mentors, training certification, and performance support tools.

The program has three phases: mentoring, the Virtual University, and leader-led classroom-based orientation. The mentoring program affords time for learners to meet with experts one-on-one and links learners with mem-

---

Five Lessons from Ford

Five guidelines for dealing with external vendors to build your e-learning program can be gleaned from the Ford experience:

1. *Know who your vendors are.* Check references, view samples, ask other customers. There's nothing worse than hiring a vendor who will be out of business by the time the project ends.
2. *Be sure you understand your technological requirements and capabilities.* Then communicate them clearly to all your potential vendors. Often, you may know what your requirements are, but until you put it down on paper, the vendor can only guess or will try to sell you his or her own solution to your problem.
3. *Make sure you have a qualified project manager.* You want someone who knows about the project and appropriate project management techniques. Don't change project managers throughout the project. Consistency is the key to success. If you don't have a strong project manager on staff, consider hiring one. The results will make up for any increase in overhead costs. (We'll discuss this in more detail in Chapter Ten.)
4. *Ensure the communication lines are opened early.* And then be sure that they stay open throughout the project. Talk to all the key players regularly. Weekly status meetings are a good forum for this. Relay any problems or issues to the project manager as soon as they occur. Proactive planning is a lot more productive than reactive scrambling.
5. *Try out all the products before buying.* Have the vendor build prototypes and test them on your systems and learners early. This eliminates problems at the end—when you don't want them.

---

bers of the sales management team, who answer questions throughout the program. The mentoring program provides a bridge in the eight-week training program between e-learning and classroom activities. The mentoring phase includes onsite orientation, with mentors facilitating the orientation sessions.

The Virtual University (VU) hosts the majority of the technical information in the training program. The VU provides media-rich WBT, a learning management system, assessment, and Internet links to presentation and discussion tools. The WBT materials are easy to update and they are accessible from any desktop continent-wide. Leader-led instruction is used to teach writing, presentation techniques, and selling skills. Leader-led instruction also includes role-playing exercises.

Real World

To simulate the real job, homework assignments mimic real problems faced by salespeople who sell complex Internet products and services. (This is a type of performance support tool.) The learners access product print guides on the company's Knowledge Bank and use this information for homework assignments. They also gain valuable role-playing experience in a Web-based training (WBT) environment by practicing sales techniques on a variety of customer personalities and in numerous scenarios. An informal learning aspect of the program employs video clips to simulate customer scenarios. The learners work their way through a series of choices, to which the customer reacts in either a positive or negative way. The scenario continues until learners win or lose their sales, based on their choices.

Throughout, the mentoring helps to link learning to the real job. By showing learners how everything in the training program relates to the real world, mentoring encourages application questions and helps to put everything in the context of the work to be performed.

Verizon's biggest challenge was to have the training program ready for hiring the first of approximately two hundred new sales representatives within four to six months. It took three months to develop the first set of modules. Within six months, on schedule, modules for eighteen hours of classroom time were completed.

Technology

Another challenge was to ensure that technology would help learning, not hamper it. Verizon quickly realized that if they were not careful when developing e-learning and if they became too dependent on high-level technology, some learners who did not have access to that level of technology would not receive the full benefit of the training. In response to that challenge, provisions were made for users who did not have access to sufficient bandwidth to take a special path to access a portion of the training. As a first step, they used paper-based materials, not e-learning. As a second step, they viewed the remaining content on the higher bandwidth LAN at a later time—e-learning.

Benefits

To determine the financial benefits of the program, two performance criteria were set: the average time it took new salespeople to close their first sale and the average dollar value of that sale. The evaluation was based on a comparison of the performance of new hires who had received the training with the performance of the representatives hired a year before who had not received the new training. The results were impressive. There was a reduction of 25 percent in the average time it took new sales representatives to produce their first sale. In addition, the average dollar value of a first sale more than doubled. Salespeople also sold more complex products and services more quickly after the new training program.

Four Lessons from Verizon

Based on their experience with e-learning, here are four recommendations from the Verizon e-learning project leaders:

- *Assess the latest learning technologies on an ongoing basis.* The field is changing day by day, and you must keep up to ensure you are incorporating the most suitable offerings into your program.
- *Be ready to mix and match the four e-learning types.* Leader-led distance learning is excellent for collaboration. Self-study formats deliver a clear message effectively and efficiently. Email and threaded discussions can support classroom training and classroom activities during or after a classroom session.
- *Plan carefully.* Take a step-by-step approach to implementing your plan.
- *Evaluate the effectiveness of the e-learning program.* Monitor expenditures. Report to stakeholders on the organizational impact.

Banking

The financial industry has also begun to experiment with the potential of e-learning.

Bank of Montreal

At the Bank of Montreal in Toronto, a multi-million-dollar learning centre is used to help bank employees learn the basics of credit transactions, investment banking, and other essential services.[16]

The bank's 33,000 employees previously received training in the old-fashioned way (as many still do), but the advent of the new learning centre has seen e-learning playing a much larger role in the training and education of bank employees. Employing a learning centre concept (a learning centre is a site away from the traditional workspace that employees can use to participate in e-learning in quiet and without interruption), the bank says it tries to incorporate some e-learning into every course it develops. All of this doesn't come cheaply however. The bank's Institute for Learning employs between 85 and 120 people and cost $50 million (Canadian) to build—not including the ongoing maintenance involved in the technology or the course development process.

Performance Support at American Express

American Express Financial Advisors in Minneapolis, Minnesota, has taken e-learning one step further. The company, which serves as a clearinghouse for American Express investment products and portfolios, has turned to technology to help it improve the ability of its customer service representatives (CSRs) to handle customer inquiries.[17] Using their electronic performance support system (EPSS), the company was able to help its CSRs alleviate the need to memorize complex rules, statutes, and regulations and to help customers wade through the bureaucratic nightmare of investment portfolios and transactions.

For example, one of the problems the CSRs dealt with was the settling of accounts upon the death of a client. If the portfolio included a mutual fund, a few stocks, and some other investment products, the customer was forced to deal with a separate CSR to resolve each issue. Furthermore, there was no system by which CSRs could view the status of other investments in the portfolio, nor were they able to assist one another in any way, as the complex rules for each product made it next to impossible to cross-train them. The result was often frustrated customers and high burnout among CSRs. The obvious solution was to connect each CSR to a computer terminal linked to the main server, which contained all the information the customer might request. The only problem was that CSRs didn't know how to access this information. The EPSS provided the CSR with a job aid that guided them through the process on demand. Now, when they are dealing with a mutual fund question and the customer also requests information on a stock issue, the CSR is able to punch a few keys or click a few screens to bring up an electronic wizard or prompt that guides him or her through the process the customer wishes to discuss. In effect, the EPSS provides the worker with learning on demand—a major advantage of the e-learning tool set.

A Glimpse Forward and Back

What have we learned about e-learning from the examples discussed in this chapter? Quite a few themes have come out, and they will be the focus of the remaining pages of this book. Effective e-learning requires:

- *A clear need and rationale.* In all of the cases we examined, there was a clear reason for implementing e-learning. A needs assessment was conducted, and a clearly defined problem that could be solved by e-learning was identified. Without a problem to address, e-learning is simply an expensive experiment.
- *Systematic design and development.* A complete course design and development process was conducted in every case. e-Learning is more than just

converting your MS Word documents to HTML or PDF and posting them on the Internet or the company intranet. To be effective, e-learning will require a complete analysis of the course or courses to be converted. This will take time to do correctly, so don't expect to see results in a couple of days.

- *In-depth knowledge of the target learners.* Each example had a clearly defined picture of the intended audience. This can be done during your initial analysis, but you should always keep it in focus. e-Learning that cannot be used by your learners won't be of much value.
- *An appropriate mix of methods.* e-Learning can be formal or informal, leader-led or self-paced, synchronous or asynchronous, and even combined with conventional methods. Whatever options you choose, remember that the end product must keep learners motivated and stimulate critical thought or demonstrate the desired outcome.
- *Skilled and motivated program designers, instructors, and managers.* Successful e-learning projects require a team of specialists. It is not something you can do by yourself. Many of the companies described used external resources to augment internal specialists. This is probably the reality of e-learning. Unless you work for Microsoft or IBM, it is doubtful you'll have everyone you need on the payroll to build a successful program.

In Part Two we will elaborate on many of these themes to give you a complete picture of how to build and conduct a successful e-learning program.

Test Drive

At the beginning of this chapter we suggested that you read each case carefully, thinking about how it reflects your own organization. You were to ask yourself whether the same issues exist in your company or institution. Are the solutions acceptable? Can you avoid the same mistakes? If so, how?

We included a summary of lessons learned from the case studies. We suggest that you use this information to build your own checklist of issues to address during e-learning implementation. Do you see additional lessons? Which ones will be crucial in your organization?

TAKING THE CHALLENGE

Frameworks for Success

Now we get into the practical aspects of planning and implementing e-learning programs. We start with "The Big Picture," a systems overview of the process, and continue through all the design, delivery, and evaluation challenges you are likely to face in implementing e-learning in any type of organization.

Specific topics covered in Part Two are

- e-Learning project management
- Assessment of e-learning needs and readiness
- Learning theory and frameworks for e-learning design and development
- Selecting e-learning courses and vendors
- e-Learning delivery
- Leading organizations when they move to e-learning
- Measuring and improving e-learning programs

CHAPTER FOUR

THE BIG PICTURE

Approaches to Project Management

Are you ready to tackle a difficult project that will require an elaborate work plan? Most likely it will test your mastery of adult learning theory and practice, as well as your leadership in instructional design, championing, managing change, managing risk, and managing consultants. Using the systems elaborated in this chapter will help e-learning leaders—whether instructors, developers, or managers—succeed.

This chapter is an overview of how e-learning programs can be developed and managed, from assessing the organization's readiness and conducting needs analyses through implementation, evaluation, and redesign. It presents the conceptual grounding for the chapters to follow, which explore assessment, design, delivery, management, and evaluation issues in more depth. This is not just a theoretical overview of e-learning project management. It stems from hands-on experience. You will also find much practical information and advice, including:

- Two step-by-step methodologies for creating and managing e-learning programs
- Sample work plans for e-learning projects
- Guidelines for writing convincing project proposals
- Quick tips on project management for quality and success

This chapter summarizes important lessons learned about leading e-learning projects and courses from a wide variety of organizations. By adapting these lessons to your own experience and developing preferred approaches for your own organization, you will be able to avoid some of the common pitfalls of managing e-learning projects and enjoy more of the benefits.

Two Project Management Approaches

The creation of e-learning programs can be viewed from two perspectives: *instructional design* and *program management*. The instructional design approach, as examined here, revolves around an eight-step instructional design and development process. The second perspective, a program management approach, involves a comprehensive seventeen-step management process. Managers, developers, and sometimes instructors use both of these processes to create and operate successful e-learning programs.

An ISD Approach

One of the best project management tools remains a simple work plan spelling out each step, individual responsibilities, and time allocated for each task, based on an instructional systems design (ISD) model. Unquestionably, some ISD processes can become convoluted and self-serving, and some of the criticism aimed in ISD's direction is earned. Complex ISD models can be counterproductive. But a simple ISD process—with steps such as scope the project, analyze, design, develop, pilot test, deliver, evaluate, and maintain—makes sense from an overall project management perspective.

Our recommended ISD process, shown in Figure 4.1, is a template for developing a solid e-learning work plan. In addition to the eight steps, beginning with project scoping and continuing through evaluation and maintenance, our diagram indicates eight decision points where the e-learning manager or instructional designer consults with the client. These decision points are opportunities to explain ideas, to check understanding, and to forge strategies. Decisions are the Achilles heel of our ISD model. They must be made carefully, with sufficient information, and they need to be clear, concise, and well-documented. Make the wrong decisions and you will cripple your e-learning effort.

FIGURE 4.1. AN EIGHT-STEP E-LEARNING DEVELOPMENT CYCLE.

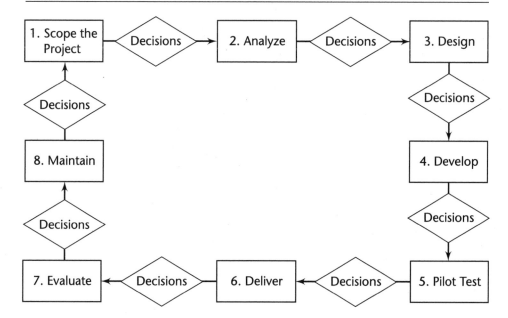

This entire book is built around an instructional systems design approach, so the elements of ISD are explained throughout the book. We will not repeat here what is said in other chapters. Rather, we will give an overview of ISD.

1. Scope the Project. The *project scoping* phase consists of general data collection to assess the feasibility of introducing e-learning in an organization. (See Chapter Five, which gives details of assessing an organization's readiness for e-learning.) The end result of this phase is a report to stakeholders that explains high-level findings about the suitability of introducing e-learning in the organization. A well-developed project scope presents a plan that the training team will follow to implement e-learning.

At the end of the project scoping phase, the training team presents a report to stakeholders that contains:

- An explanation of the methods followed in the project scoping phase
- An outline of data collected
- An interpretation of the data, with emphasis on the suitability of e-learning in the particular environment

- An analysis of the costs and benefits associated with the recommendations
- Clear recommendations about the next steps to take

If e-learning is recommended and approved, the project goes to the next step, instructional analysis.

2. Analyze. Instructional *analysis* provides the information that is required to make sound decisions about the content and methods of the e-learning program. The seven types of instructional analysis (context, technology, users, work, training suitability, content, and cost/benefit) are examined in depth in Chapter Five.

3. Design. *Design* refers to planning the e-learning course and materials. In Chapter Six we review design in detail. The design ideas of Robert Gagné are discussed at some length, as they present a model for effective e-learning design. In the design stage, the instructional design team lays out the curriculum, selects training methodologies, and sets the objectives for the training modules. The design phase also includes the development of a small segment of the e-learning as a model or prototype for review.

4. Develop. In the *development* phase, training developers implement what was planned in the design phase in terms of curriculum, methodologies, and objectives, together with what they learned and gained agreement on during prototyping. Quality control and ad hoc internal reviews by clients and colleagues should be completed in the development phase. Chapter Seven deals with development.

5. Pilot Test. Once some materials are developed, they are reviewed with users and stakeholders in pilot instructional sessions. Pilot testing helps to ensure that the training works well in the conditions under which it will be used eventually.

Alpha Testing. When designing any type of training, especially e-learning, it is essential to test whether what is being crafted functions effectively on various types of hardware and with the typical users. An *alpha test* refers to the process of subjecting training materials to internal testing, that is, testing conducted by people who work on the project or who are near to the design team. Alpha testing helps to ensure that stakeholders commit to the design before costly development continues. Alpha testing can start in the design and development phases and continue into the pilot testing phase.

Beta Testing. Beta testing *is also carried out in the pilot testing phase. An effective beta test meets the following conditions:*

- Developers deliver the pilot session to an audience that is representative of the target audience
- Representatives from the client and from the development team observe the pilot
- Following the pilot, participants are debriefed to gather their reactions
- Based on the observations, the team identifies areas for improvement
- When approved, these recommendations are incorporated into the final materials

6. Deliver. *Delivery* or presentation consists of using the material in a learning situation. During this step, the materials are still being assessed. Feedback and observation can provide data for improving the materials. Chapter Eight deals with the delivery of e-learning.

7. Evaluate. *Evaluation* helps developers to draw accurate conclusions about the impact of e-learning. Evaluations tell them whether the original needs assessment was accurate and whether the program design is appropriate. Were the learning objectives well-chosen? Did participants learn what was intended? Has the organization benefited from the training? Chapter Ten deals with e-learning evaluation at considerable length.

8. Maintain. Ongoing maintenance of e-learning ensures that materials, instructional strategies, and exercises are updated and that users' comments are addressed.

The Pros and Cons of ISD. ISD today is the center of a heated discussion similar in some ways to the "Is God dead?" debate of earlier decades: in certain circles ISD is considered dead. ISD doomsayers insist that ISD has become linear, discrete, terminal, sequential, and driven by one subject-matter expert. An ISD-based program could show these characteristics—but this need not be the case. ISD is a tool, and like any tool it can be misused. ISD proponents see the process as dynamic, flexible, and multifaceted; in the hands of experienced designers the steps are not linear, discrete, terminal, sequential, or driven by one subject-matter expert. Experienced ISD practitioners modify ISD previous lessons in the same way that artists build on the subjects and techniques of past masters, and thus the practitioners continue to grow, adapt, and learn throughout their lives.

A Way of Thinking. ISD is not a flow chart. It is a way of thinking: a commitment to systematically, broadly, reflectively—and sometimes slowly, or should I say deliberately—designing training, or not designing training if it is not the right approach. It takes time to develop excellent training programs. ISD-driven training development takes time, but in the hands of a skilled developer, ISD gets results.

Integrated, Not Fragmented. When we divide a complex process like training design into eight steps as we have above, we can grasp the separate elements of the instruction cycle. That's the good news. In that sense it helps to understand the complexity of ISD. However, this fragmentation of a dynamic process can be misleading. In fact, the steps are not discrete entities as the model in Figure 4.1 suggests. The processes intersect, overlap, and interact with each other. Together they generate a synergistic effect: one propels the other. The successful completion of one engenders positive results in another step—or all other steps. All the phases are part of one entity—an integrated whole. They build on each other. The whole is greater than the sum of its parts.

A Plan of Action. The eight-step ISD process is not an instant, just add water and stir, recipe for designing instruction. Rather, it is a roadmap for a long, perhaps challenging journey. Your client sets the destination on any given instructional design project—whether you are a training manager or an instructional designer. During the voyage, you do the driving, in full consultation with the "back-seat driver" client. You may have to climb hills, make detours, and generally adapt to the terrain. You might need to slam on the brakes from time to time, bring your journey to a sudden halt, and take stock of progress to date—as measured by your client. At times you will have to push the pedal to the metal to make up for lost time. Your vehicle might need to be repaired or tuned. And most certainly, you will have to "fill 'er up" along the way.

In other words, our ISD model is a generic plan of action. You will have to adapt it with intelligent flexibility, slowing down and speeding up as required by circumstances. The success of your e-learning project will probably ultimately depend on the extent to which you came to a mutual understanding with your stakeholders about the process you are following.

Developing a Work Plan from the ISD Diagram. Figure 4.2 illustrates a typical work plan developed from the eight-step ISD model. In the figure, we have expanded the first phase, as an illustration of how each of the phases needs to be expanded. The seven additional steps for each phase are

1. Develop the process for the business of each phase.
2. Submit the process for review.
3. Revise as necessary.
4. Finalize.
5. Conduct.
6. Report.
7. Finalize results.

In other words, within each phase there is a sequence of steps whereby the leader and the client agree on the process, the work is carried out, the work is presented to the client for approval, it is revised as necessary, and the project scope is finalized. In a complete ISD work plan, all eight phases would contain the type of detail shown for the project scoping phase in Figure 4.2.

Tips for Making ISD a Valuable Tool. A project plan with an embedded ISD process is not just a theoretical document. It is a tool to focus energy, meet deadlines, and find solutions. When used hand in hand with project management processes, ISD is a systematic, logical process for chunking large challenges into manageable tasks. Whether you are using the eight-step ISD process or the more detailed seventeen-step program management model, explained later, keep in mind some of the lessons others have learned from managing e-learning projects.

FIGURE 4.2. ISD MODEL WORK PLAN.

Elements	Weeks

Elements	1	2	3	4	5	6	7	8	9	10	11	12	13	14	15	16	17	18	19	20	21	22
1. Scope the project	■	■	■	■																		
1.1 Develop scoping process	■																					
1.2 Submit scoping process	■																					
1.3 Revise as necessary		■																				
1.4 Finalize		■																				
1.5 Conduct scoping		■																				
1.6 Report on scoping			■																			
1.7 Finalize scoping results				■																		
2. Analyze					■																	
3. Design						■	■	■														
4. Develop									■	■	■	■	■									
5. Pilot test													■									
6. Deliver														■	■	■	■	■	■	■	■	■
7. Evaluate																	■	■	■			
8. Maintain																			■	■	■	■

- Learn as much as possible about the project before committing to a work plan.
- Build review time into a plan for commenting on work throughout the project.
- Make a clear distinction in your mind and in your plans between *effort* (the number of days to devote to completing the work) and *duration* (the amount of time to complete the project, including review).
- Once a work plan has been approved, stick to it; if revisions are necessary, make them formally—in writing.
- When completing a task, keep a scrupulous record of how much time it takes. You will be able to use this information next time in your estimates.

Lessons from Our Experience

Having worked on several e-learning implementation projects, we have noticed the following themes:

- Implementing e-learning is complex
- Most organizations are still experimenting with e-learning
- Organizations are using a variety of approaches for implementing e-learning
- Implementing e-learning means far more than subscribing to the courses of a service provider
- Implementing e-learning is about project management, change management, and risk management

---

A Broad Approach to Program Development

The eight-step ISD process is the skeleton for developing an e-learning project management work plan. The eight steps are more appropriate for a course development project, while a broader process is better applied at the program development level.

This broader approach is based on the idea that seventeen elements must be considered in developing and designing e-learning programs overall. As illustrated in Tables 4.1 through 4.4, these elements become steps for successful program management. These seventeen steps are not intended to be a rigorous roadmap that you stray from at your peril—like a path through the jungle. Rather, this is an approach that can be adapted to your particular situation. In this journey, you can change lanes if you wish.

The seventeen steps are divided into four phases: (1) getting ready, (2) establishing the framework, (3) high-level implementation, and (4) looking after the details. The steps are presented within each phase in order of precedence, with the idea that the first one is normally started before the second one, and so forth. However, this is not a linear, step-by-step formula. Multi-tasking e-learning program developers and managers are required to undertake several of these steps at the same time. In your organization, one step might be more important than another. As a result, you might change the order of the steps.

Phase One: Getting Ready. You must do your homework before launching an e-learning program. Prepare yourself. Create and clarify the management structures, identify how people learn best, plug yourself into the latest research about e-learning, and grasp the context of implementing e-learning in your organization. Information you gather about these four areas will help you to understand the high-level direction of e-learning. This phase provides the first level of information that will help your organization decide whether e-learning is feasible for you. See Table 4.1 for the steps within Phase One.

TABLE 4.1. PHASE ONE: GETTING READY.

Element	Actions	Examples
1. Management	Define structure of coordinating body. Articulate roles and responsibilities. Select champions. Explain management business framework to all stakeholders.	Bank One managed e-learning through a fifty-member cross-functional team. Cisco and Dell created e-learning councils of leaders.
2. Learners	Determine how they learn best. Identify their performance gaps, experiences, and expectations.	Several organizations, including the Canadian Army, have been surprised to learn that students were missing basic skills they needed to use e-learning materials. A questionnaire can help to identify these gaps.
3. Research on e-learning	Explore research and anecdotal information to determine how to implement e-learning successfully in your environment. Explain findings to main stakeholders.	Web sites of Brandon Hall (www.brandon-hall.com) and Elliot Masie (www.masie.com) offer free anecdotal information about e-learning. The ASTD site (www.astd.org) provides free benchmarking information about e-learning.
4. Context	Identify driving and restraining forces for the acceptance of e-learning. Identify steps needed to attenuate the restraining forces. Explain findings to main stakeholders.	In the larger business context, e-learning is part of e-commerce. Many companies are driven to e-learning by mergers.

Phase Two: Establish the Framework. In the second phase, you will need to do some serious thinking about using technology, building your business case, selecting your business model, and handling evaluation issues. These elements will help you to gain approval from stakeholders and establish a firm foundation for your e-learning program. See Table 4.2 for an outline of this phase.

TABLE 4.2. PHASE TWO: ESTABLISHING THE FRAMEWORK.

Element	Actions	Examples
5. Technology	Identify what technology is available, what technology will be needed, and the role of standards such as learning objects. Develop a relationship with your technical advisors.	Domino's Pizza chose CBT on CD-ROM, not WBT over the Web, because their franchisees did not have Web access. Cisco converted six LMS systems gained through mergers to one.
6. Business case	Identify the why, what, how of implementing e-learning in business terms. Provide estimated costs and cost savings. Obtain approval for a phased project.	For IBM the business case was based on the argument that there was no other way to train thirty thousand employees in new business practices quickly. Air Canada focused on safety training. Rockwell Collins' business case was based on getting products to market faster.
7. Business model	Select the best model or models: integrated or decentralized, minimal or optimal, make or buy, independent or cooperative, national or international.	Cisco started small with two thousand members of a sales group. Shell decided that the business model of e-learning is that it is not learning. It is not knowledge management. It is business. The Canadian military is starting with an extensive test site that they call a proof of concept.
8. Evaluation	Develop an evaluation strategy, some instruments, and the reports; then determine how evaluation results will be used with each phase.	The Canadian military adapted the benchmarking study of the Institute for Higher Education policy called *Quality on the Line*.

Phase Three: High-Level Implementation. You have now decided to move forward with e-learning. Your focus switches from explanation and justification to high-level implementation. As you move ahead, you should concentrate on communication, administration, content, and methodologies.

TABLE 4.3. PHASE THREE: HIGH-LEVEL IMPLEMENTATION.

Element	Actions	Examples
9. Communication	Identify who communicates with whom, how, what, and when. Identify what questions people have about e-learning. Build a change management strategy to answer people's questions about the new initiative.	INCO set up an intranet site to answer questions about e-learning. Dell sends e-magnets to employees announcing information about the e-learning program. IBM used the outside/inside approach to communication by going public with articles and presentations about the program.
10. Administration	Set up the administration. Define the need for data on participation and for follow-up mechanisms. Determine which LMS is best for this role.	When the Canadian Army introduced e-learning, they found that administrative staff needed to develop new skills. Training programs were developed to achieve this. Participants are taught how to carry out their administrative tasks using the learning management system.
11. Content	Identify what needs to be taught and developed, both internally and externally.	Many organizations start by subscribing to service providers such as SmartForce, NETg, or ElementK. They measure usage and reaction and decide from there what else to implement.
12. Methodologies	Based on information collected thus far, select training methodologies. Identify extent of blending of conventional and e-learning. Select from four types of e-learning (informal, self-directed, instructor-led, and performance support tools).	The Canadian military has leader-led and self-paced e-learning. Shell has a heavy knowledge management component to their e-learning, as do many high-tech firms where employees need to access technical information about new products quickly.

Phase Four: Looking After the Details. Throughout an e-learning project, there are plenty of details that require attention. They are important throughout a project, but even more important in the later stages when the project is exposed to the scrutiny of stakeholders and users. There is important work to do associated with human resources, selecting a starting point, implementing, evaluating, and constantly re-jigging your approaches (see Table 4.4).

TABLE 4.4. PHASE FOUR: LOOKING AFTER THE DETAILS.

Element	Actions	Examples
13. Human resources	Identify the required skills given the present capacity of the organization and develop an approach (train, recruit, or contract out) to acquire the necessary resources.	The U.S. Coast Guard found there was a need for additional administrative personnel to manage e-learning. The Canadian military developed a program to train online facilitators.
14. Starting point	Identify which topics are best to teach at the beginning in order to foster high levels of usage, understanding, and buy-in. There is an opportunity here to do something innovative. Follow the pain; find a topic that is not taught now and can be taught successfully with e-learning.	Air Canada started with safety training and saved money from not printing manuals and also reached a large audience.
15. Implement	Launch carefully. Communicate extensively with all users: learners, supervisors, instructors, and managers.	From the start of the project to this step, IBM and other organizations took a year or more. Most organizations target a 60 to 80 percent solution at this time, knowing that they will have to revise their approach over time.

Element	Actions	Examples
16. Evaluate	Conduct an evaluation with quantitative and qualitative data.	The Canadian Army implemented a pilot e-learning program and conducted an extensive evaluation. Using quantitative data from questionnaires and qualitative data from focus groups, the evaluators identified many lessons learned.
17. Re-jig	Continually review progress and revise items 1 through 16 above as required.	Implementing e-learning is an ongoing process. Re-jigging involves consulting with the management group, revisiting all the steps in the process, and making modifications based on the evaluation.

A Seventeen-Step Work Plan

Figure 4.3 converts the seventeen-step process, just discussed, into a work plan. In the illustration, the project has been compressed into a twenty-two-week period. But projects often take twice as long as that—or longer—depending on the organization's complexity, capacity, and level of conviction. Also, depending on the exact situation and the competencies of the people assigned to the project, achieving all of the work illustrated here will require several people to work full-time for the twenty-two weeks. This is a high-level plan and it has to be broken down into more detail before it can be used. Within each of the seventeen phases, steps are required whereby the leader and the client agree on the process, the work is carried out, the work is presented to the client for approval, the plan is revised as necessary, and the plan is finalized. An example of a more detailed breakdown is contained in the work plan developed earlier in the chapter in conjunction with an ISD model, where we broke the first phase into seven steps.

FIGURE 4.3. SAMPLE SEVENTEEN-STEP WORK PLAN.

Elements	Weeks
	1 2 3 4 5 6 7 8 9 10 11 12 13 14 15 16 17 18 19 20 21 22
1. Establish management	
2. Research learners	
3. Investigate e-learning	
4. Establish context	
5. Investigate technology	
6. Establish business case	
7. Establish business model	
8. Plan evaluation	
9. Plan communications	
10. Set up administration	
11. Establish content	
12. Select methodologies	
13. Manage human resources	
14. Establish starting point	
15. Implement	
16. Evaluate	
17. Re-jig	

Components of a Convincing Proposal

When you have completed your analysis, whether you are using the eight-step ISD process or the seventeen-step project management process, it is time to write a proposal. Your thorough research and clear analysis will not amount to anything unless you are able to communicate your results clearly. People listening to your presentation or reading your proposal will find you more credible if you follow a systematic reasoning process. The eight elements laid out below can help you to convey your thoughts clearly.

1. Purpose, Goal, or Statement of Issue. The purpose, goal, or issue statement explains what you intend to do when investigating e-learning. *Example:* "We undertook to determine the potential use of e-learning at the ACME manufacturing plant to train furniture technicians on safe practices for wood finishing."

2. Research Question. A research question is a clear statement of the problem that you are attempting to solve. Your clarity will help to convince readers and listeners of your insight. *Example:* "We set out to determine the content and supporting technology for a training program to train furniture technicians at six plants on safe practices for wood finishing."

3. Conceptual Framework. When you think through an issue, you use words and concepts. The same words might be given different meaning in another situation or in another country. In a written proposal or oral presentation, you have to explain the meaning given to terms such as e-learning or online learning, as well as other key concepts. Otherwise, your advice will be confusing, not convincing. *Example:* "We used a broad definition of e-learning

---

Making a Proposal Convincing

We can convince with both logic and passion. If you believe strongly, your passion will show through. And passion should show. Reason is also necessary. Our eight components hinge on reason and clarity. You provide the passion. We outline the basic content for you to cover. You will have to decide the depth of analysis and formality that is appropriate for the organization where you are making your proposal.

that includes all forms of technology-assisted learning, including computer-based training, Web-based training, and all forms of leader-led and self-paced learning."

4. Assumptions. In every situation, we hold assumptions that guide our views, methods of investigation, and conclusions. In our example, we will have to make assumptions about such matters as the budget, the number of participants, and the availability of hardware. In a convincing proposal we need to explain these assumptions. *Example:* "The proposal is based on the following assumptions: the budget for the development of the training is $150,000; the goal is to train six hundred workers; and all participants will have access to a multimedia computer."

5. Methods. It is important to explain to readers and listeners how you collected data and arrived at conclusions. For example, you could explain that you decided to conduct interviews as the best way to collect spontaneous information. You could outline the topics covered in the interviews, the number conducted, and the general results of the process. *Example:* "We held individual interviews with ten management stakeholders and held four focus groups with five operational employees in each group. We asked the individuals and the focus group members what had been their personal experiences with technology-assisted learning and what had been the experience of the organization with technology-assisted learning to date."

6. Data Collected. An overview of the data collected, analyzed in a meaningful manner, is a powerful way to engage readers and listeners in the process you followed to arrive at your conclusions. The report could include facts such as the extent of experience that potential learners have had to date with e-learning. *Example:* "We found that all supervisors have experience with e-learning. They all indicated that e-learning has been a positive experience for them. However, at least 50 percent of the operational staff have no experience with e-learning, and many have no experience with computers."

7. Graphics. Graphics are a good way to summarize your research and present your conclusions. *Example:* "See Figure 4.4, which presents the learners' previous experience with e-learning as a bar graph."

FIGURE 4.4. SAMPLE GRAPHIC TO ACCOMPANY PROPOSAL.

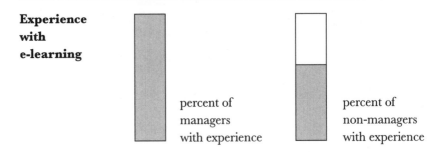

**Experience
with
e-learning**

percent of
managers
with experience

percent of
non-managers
with experience

8. Business Case. What deductions can one draw from your data? How do these deductions compare with other interpretations drawn by other researchers? How do they compare with the literature on the topic or with benchmarking studies? How will these conclusions help the business position of ACME? Business case. Business case. Business case. Remember that successful e-learning is about defining your business case and developing an approach to meet business needs. *Example:* "We found five studies where industry had used e-learning to train workers in safe working practices. Three of these paralleled the technology we envisage using at ACME. In all cases the budget was similar to the one we plan to use and, in the end, with e-learning the companies delivered the accident prevention at a 25 percent savings, and the safety record of the companies in the area being taught remained stable."

Elements of a Comprehensive Development Plan

After you have your work plan and your proposal, you must develop an implementation plan. A thorough e-learning implementation plan includes information on the following:

- Program sponsor and staff
- Thrust of program
- Types of training materials
- Instruction methods
- Presentation methods

- Distribution methods
- Follow-up procedures
- Initial assumptions about key issues
- Key participants
- Project risks

These elements are listed in Table 4.5, which can be used as a checklist to plan an e-learning project. Sample responses have been filled in.

TABLE 4.5. SAMPLE E-LEARNING PROJECT PLAN.

Criteria	Sample Response
Program Profile	
Name of project	*ERP implementation at ACME Industries*
Project sponsor	*Ted Techie, director of information services*
Training lead	*Tina Trainer, director of training*
Who will take the program?	*1,500 employees*
Jobs of participants	*Operational and supervisory*
Location of participants	*All six plants in the region*
Thrust of Program	
Information	*Employees will receive before training in newsletter*
Education	*Before training in a desk drop*
Training	*Hands-on during course*
General content of program	*Key functions of ERPsoft that targeted ACME employees will use in their work*
Curriculum of program	*Comparison to existing software, logon, navigation, requisitions, work planning*
Types of Training Materials	
Custom designed	*For work planning*
Off-the-shelf	*For logon, navigation requisitions (to be purchased from ERPsoft)*
Instruction Methods	
Case studies	*For requisitioning and work planning*
Reading	*For the list of employer codes*
Discussion	*For comparing the existing and new software*
Group work	*For verifying the accuracy of input*
Coaching	*To ensure personal commitment*
Job aids	*For main keyboard commands*

Criteria	Sample Response
Presentation Methods	
e-Learning	*Mailing list and virtual community*
Audio	*Used in the CD-ROM*
Video	*Used in the CD-ROM*
Online help	*Has been developed for ERPsoft and the training will be based on the information contained therein*
Other	*Students will be given the option of taking the training in a leader-led classroom*
Distribution Methods	
CD-ROM	*One for the entire program to be given to each employee*
Intranet	*Will be offered where it is available, and the CD-ROM will be converted to be used in html on the intranet*
Email	*Will be used to provide updated documentation*
Bulletin board	*Will be used in the intranet version for participants to raise issues and post best practices*
Other	*Paper-based handouts will be distributed in the leader-led classroom version of the program*
Follow-Up to Training	
After go live	*Instructors will circulate in the workplace for two weeks after go live*
Plan for acquiring or producing the materials	*Acquired within four weeks of approving the plan/produced within eight weeks of plan approval*
Initial Assumptions About Key Issues	
System	*The system will be ready four weeks before training starts so materials can be finalized*
Content	*The content is as identified by ACME subject-matter experts*
Learners	*They will have the prerequisite knowledge of MS Windows that is required to participate fully in the ERPsoft training sessions*
Resources	*Will require two instructional designers for two months and two developers to work in Toolbook*
Facilities	*Four classrooms will be available full-time for training over a three-week period before go live and for five weeks after go live*
Stakeholders	*Ted Techie, director of information services, is the key stakeholder and will facilitate the review and approval of key deliverables*

Criteria	Sample Response
Key Participants	
Subject-matter experts	*Pat Pringle, Jean Belleville*
Designers	*Rose Trimble, Jack Madison*
Instructors	*To be selected from the ACME workforce*
Project Risks	
Tight timeframes	*Need to carefully plan how long it will take based on the time it takes to prototype materials; once prototyping is completed, the resulting work plan must be monitored closely*
Everyone must be available as indicated in the work plan	*Project lead must plan availability and monitor it closely*
All training rooms must be allocated to this project as planned	*Project lead has to plan the availability of training rooms and monitor it closely*
Training work stations must be installed one week before training starts	*Project lead has to plan the availability of training rooms and monitor it closely*
A fixed price budget, explained in a separate document	*Project could go over budget if deadlines are missed, so project lead must monitor budget closely*

Note: The information contained in this analysis was accurate at the time it was written. Changes in the depth or breadth of the content, number of trainees, or timetable could affect the final timeframes and the final costs.

Signatures

Sponsor: _____ Date: _____

Training Lead: _____ Date: _____

Ten Quick Tips for Project Quality and Success

Whether you are an internal consultant or an external one, people you work with will be expecting results. One way to show results is to manage projects effectively. Here are ten tips on how to develop and manage an e-learning project for quality and success. You can use the form in Table 4.6 to measure current performance for yourself, others, or an entire organization.

1. *Develop your project management skills.* If there are gaps in your knowledge, learn about instructional design techniques, project management software, and training needs analysis techniques. Choose from the large variety of good courses, tutorials, and books. Free, detailed information about project planning is available at the Web site of the Project Planning Institute at www.pmi.com.

2. *Take time to gather background information.* Learn as much as possible about the organization and about the context of the project before committing to a work plan.

3. *Write the contract carefully.* Internal or external clients are often not certain what they want or need. When your clients or colleagues do not know what they expect, you can't be certain how long it will take to complete the work. Under such circumstances, avoid a fixed duration commitment or contract. Instead, opt for a phased project in which you do a piece of work and then estimate the next phase based on the amount of time it took for the last one. If you are an external consultant, a day-to-day contract works well, where the client pays for each day of work completed, rather than paying a fixed price for completing the project deliverables.

4. *Allow for ongoing review.* Build plenty of review time into a work plan, so stakeholders who are required to give you feedback can critique your work at different stages.

5. *Understand the importance of effort versus duration.* Make a clear distinction in your mind and on your written plans between effort (the number of days you need to devote to completing the work) and duration (the amount of time to complete the project, including review time for the organization's approval).

6. *Take advantage of software.* Use project management software, such as Microsoft Project®, to plan your work and help forecast effort and duration. Clients, external and internal, love a clear plan.

7. *Make work plan revisions cautiously.* Once the work plan has been approved, stick to it. If revisions are necessary, make them formally.

8. *Hone your word processing skills.* Get full value from word processing software by using automated features such as styles, templates, and graphics that will help you quickly compose spiffy status reports.

9. *Report early and often.* Make regular reports to keep all stakeholders involved in the project abreast of progress and challenges.

10. *Keep good records.* When working on a task, keep a scrupulous record of how much time it took. You will be able to use this information next time in your estimates if you have miscalculated the first time.

You may measure performance against the ten criteria described above using the assessment tool presented in Table 4.6 below.

TABLE 4.6. E-LEARNING PROJECT SUCCESS CHECKLIST.

Tips	High	Medium	Low
1. Project management skills	☐	☐	☐
2. Background information	☐	☐	☐
3. Contract precision	☐	☐	☐
4. Review time	☐	☐	☐
5. Effort versus duration	☐	☐	☐
6. Software use	☐	☐	☐
7. Revisions to work plan	☐	☐	☐
8. Word processing skills	☐	☐	☐
9. Reports to client	☐	☐	☐
10. Record keeping	☐	☐	☐

The Tasks Ahead

So much for the overview. The chapters ahead take you into the details of assessment and analysis methods, issues in e-learning design and development, selecting and delivering e-learning courses, and ideas for measuring and improving your e-learning program.

In the meantime, remember that if you are careful about your e-learning management strategy you will succeed. Watch for hazards. Keep your concentration. Pace yourself. Remember that you are not alone. Collaborate fully and carefully. Foster partnerships. Support your teammates before, during, and after the e-learning implementation race.

Test Drive

Consider the two models of e-learning implementation highlighted in this chapter. Select an organization in which e-learning could be implemented. Decide whether you should use the eight-step process or the seventeen-step one. Consider the ten tips for successful e-learning project management. Which ones will be critical in the organization you selected for implementing e-learning?

CHAPTER FIVE

ASSESSMENT AND ANALYSIS

Gauging Your Organization's Readiness

Assessing a situation before taking action can be a superficial matter or it can be very involved, depending on the circumstances. For example, golfers get a rough idea of the speed and direction of the wind by throwing a few blades of grass into the air. The path of the grass, as it falls to the ground, gives an idea of the speed and direction of the wind. This information helps golfers decide where to aim and how hard to swing a club. However, if you are flying a large airplane that is running out of fuel and you want to calculate the speed of the wind so that you can estimate how much farther you can fly, you will want to take very precise measurements of the wind velocity, the distance ahead, and other factors that will determine fuel consumption.

If you are making a major investment in e-learning, it's like flying a jet-liner in that you must have accurate information, accurate calculations, and tools you can trust. If you are not making a major investment in e-learning and are simply encouraging a few people to sign up for a distance education e-learning course, it's more like measuring the wind conditions on the golf course. You want to know which way the wind is blowing, but you don't need a precise measure of its velocity.

In this chapter, we will emphasize the kind of precise approach a pilot takes on a jetliner. We will examine seven types of data you need to collect and analyze in order to make good decisions about e-learning. We will also elaborate on a process for collecting that data and interpreting it. We know that this may be more than some readers require, so we have also included two rapid approaches: a simple five-question assessment and a quick version of a force-field analysis. In addition, we will consider lessons learned when using the tools described in this chapter.

First, the two quick ways to determine the need for e-learning.

A Five-Question Simplified Assessment

If you do not require an elaborate way to measure which way the e-learning wind is blowing, you can use the following five questions to assess needs:

1. What do people need to learn?
2. What is the best way for them to learn this: informal, self-paced, leader-led, or performance support—or, of course, a blend?
3. How could technology-assisted learning help?
4. What are the potential pitfalls with using technology?
5. How will the organization evaluate success?

These questions will generate basic information, especially in the hands of a very skilled interviewer and instructional designer, to help your organization decide whether it is ready for e-learning. But the answers will not give you everything you need to start developing an e-learning program. You will appreciate the difference when you look at the more detailed process we describe later in this chapter.

A Quick Force-Field Analysis

In addition to the five-question approach, another quick way to assess whether an organization is ready for e-learning is to gather a focus group of people who are savvy about the organization's training endeavors and ask them to identify experiences the organization has had with technology-assisted learning. Group their responses into two categories—positive and negative. Use Kurt Lewin's force-field analysis model to interpret the results. If the positives outweigh the negatives, the conclusion would be to proceed, at least to the next level of inquiry. (An example of force-field analysis as part of the comprehensive assessment process is given later in this chapter.)

The Only Show in Town?

Sometimes when we focus on a specific area such as e-learning, whether from inside or outside an organization, we lose the broader perspective: there is more to training and education than e-learning. If you have the big picture when you are collecting data, you might uncover critical information that can be used in other areas. For example, you might discover that an organization is missing basic components of a training program. For instance, the organization may lack mechanisms for developing training priorities and evaluating a learning program. Consequently, your recommendations about implementing e-learning would include ways to identify and prioritize training needs as well as approaches for evaluating all aspects of learning. With these elements in place, all learning, including e-learning, would have a better chance of succeeding. The bottom line is clear: while you are collecting information for an e-learning analysis, look for broader training and education issues and make recommendations on how they should be approached. Again, there is more to training than e-learning.

The Comprehensive Approach

And now for the detailed "jetliner approach." This comprehensive method is founded on the idea that solid facts or data, subjected to a thorough analysis, can help convince decision makers whether or not e-learning is a good option. This same data will help you develop a successful approach to e-learning when it is time to develop e-learning materials. To take the pulse of your organization and to make recommendations about e-learning, you must collect seven types of data:

- *Context data:* information about the business needs and reasons that e-learning has been suggested or is supported
- *Technology data:* the current state of technology in the organization and its suitability for e-learning

- *User data:* facts about potential participants and instructors
- *Work data:* detailed information on the tasks being performed
- *Content data:* review and analysis of the documents, procedures, industry standards, legal regulations, and other requirements applicable to the job
- *Training suitability data:* information to determine whether training is the right solution
- *Cost/benefit data:* data to calculate the cost/benefit ratio or the return on investment (ROI) of the proposed training

The reason that seven types of data must be gathered is that e-learning brings huge changes to an organization, so you need to ensure that the e-learning you develop is tooled to the needs of your organization.

Context Analysis

First, you have to understand the complexities of the organization. A context analysis will help you do this. In this initial phase of our thorough approach to needs identification, you consult decision makers, listen carefully, and generally take the pulse of the organization. Context data helps you to define what the main stakeholders hope to accomplish through e-learning.

There is a supremely practical reason for conducting a thorough context analysis. You want to understand the thinking of the key person or groups in the organization. Quite often, their opinions conflict. You must consider the wishes of all stakeholders. Your role is to collect information, sort through it, decide what makes sense, and make your recommendations based on your critical thinking.

Sample Context Analysis Questions. Here are some sample *context questions* to ask during interviews:

- Who are the decision makers?
- How can one gain access to the decision makers?
- Who decided that there should be an investigation of e-learning?
- What is the business need for the proposed e-learning?
- What can instructional developers and instructors do to ensure success when intervening in this organization?
- Are managers committed to e-learning?

- What are the preferred instructional methodologies of the organization?
- What criteria will the organization use to judge whether or not the training is successful?
- What other contextual information should you be aware of in developing e-learning?

Questions like these will help you to identify key issues, such as the reason why e-learning is being considered. Did someone have a positive experience with e-learning? Is the motivation strictly to reduce costs? Is the main reason for e-learning to allow greater access to training? What is the business case for e-learning? In other words, how will e-learning enhance the success of the organization? How much information does the organization have about e-learning?

Ideas for Analysis. Once you have collected contextual data, you have to make sense of it. There are several ways to analyze the data, ranging from a simple tabulation of the frequency of a particular response to judgments about the influence a particular respondent has in the organization or how an observation might have changed over time. Suggested criteria and sample observations and analysis are shown in Table 5.1. The same criteria can be applied to data you collect in all seven types of analysis.

TABLE 5.1. SUGGESTED CRITERIA FOR DATA ANALYSIS.

Criteria for Analysis	Data Collected and Analysis
Frequency of a particular response	Seventy-five percent of respondents indicated concern about replacing classroom courses with e-learning, leading to the decision to implement e-learning cautiously.
Consistency of responses	Two interviewers conducted separate focus groups at the same time and received similar input that learners lacked basic computer skills necessary to use e-learning, leading them to recommend computer orientation courses.
Amount of influence of the person who made the response	When senior management indicated that they felt self-paced e-learning would be too expensive, interviewers collected additional information about the cost of self-paced versus leader-led e-learning and included it in their recommendations.

Criteria for Analysis	Data Collected and Analysis
Changes in data over a period of time	An organization spread its investigation of the potential of e-learning over a period of eighteen months and found that respondents' skill levels with e-learning-related software was enhanced, thus leading them to conclude that there was an encouraging environment for the implementation of e-learning.
Criticality of the information to the success of e-learning in the organization	When IT personnel indicated in a focus group that they had major concerns about e-learning, an organization decided to undertake a detailed IT survey to obtain a complete picture of IT-related issues.

In your recommendations based on a context analysis, think critically about the implications of what you have found. For example, if you notice strong resistance, you may need to develop a comprehensive change management strategy. If you realize that the organization has had a poor track record with similar endeavors, it might be wise to recommend risk management and special project management strategies. If there are big gaps in knowledge about e-learning, you might suggest how the organization can expand its understanding. If there is little practical knowledge of e-learning, you might suggest that people take an e-learning course. Do champions have to be identified, developed, and acknowledged? Does the organization need to establish a center of e-learning expertise? What other ways could be used to concentrate efforts on moving forward? Brainstorm with colleagues, consult experts, form ad hoc advisory groups—whatever it takes to come up with creative recommendations to address the context issues your needs identification surfaces.

Technology Analysis

When it comes to deciding whether an organization is ready for e-learning, technology warrants separate consideration. For instance, plenty of computer processing power is required to use the latest features of some e-learning methods. Video, for example, requires the capacity for transferring data that comes with high bandwidth.

Sample Technology Analysis Questions. Answers to questions like the following will help you decide whether an organization's *technology* can handle e-learning:

- What has been the IT group's experience with e-learning?
- What does the IT group know about e-learning?
- How do e-learning users connect to the Web at present?
- How do users connect to their organization's network?
- If the following are used, what are their speeds: modems, Internet service provider lines, and CD-ROM drives?
- What is the current technology for supporting virtual communities (chat, listservs, threaded discussions, and so forth)?
- What are the security issues associated with e-learning in the specific organization?
- What plans does the organization have for expanding technology in one year? In two years?
- If the organization does not have the capacity or the technology to accommodate e-learning, is there an openness to go outside to an application service provider (ASP)?

Technology analysis questions help to define what type of e-learning can be delivered using the technology that the organization has. When it comes to interpreting the answers to your questions, consider the same criteria you used in your context analysis (Table 5.1). In forming your recommendations, remember that you can never be sure how the existing technology will perform once e-learning makes added demands on the system. It is often helpful to recommend a comprehensive pilot or proof of concept phase in which all aspects of e-learning are tested under actual conditions.

User Analysis

The purpose of user analysis is to obtain a clear picture of the learners and instructors who will use the e-learning materials. In some organizations, technology is king and learners and instructors have both the requisite technical skills and positive images of themselves as computer users. They will use e-learning and succeed with it. In organizations in which learners or instructors lack these qualities, e-learning will be an uphill struggle to implement. As in the other types of analyses, the criteria in Table 5.1 are a good way to begin examining your data and forming recommendations.

Sample User Analysis Questions. Here are some sample questions to ask to collect user facts. Answers will give information that you can use in proposing and developing e-learning.

- What expectations do participants and instructors have about e-learning?
- What experiences (both negative and positive) have instructors and learners had with different e-learning methods, including informal learning, self-paced, leader-led, and performance support tools?
- How much do learners and instructors know about the topic or topics to be taught?
- What are learners' and instructors' numbers, education, ages, genders, and native languages?
- How do the proposed participants prefer to learn?
- How do the instructors prefer to teach?
- When are instructors and potential participants available?

You might collect some surprising facts with the questions above. For example, if people feel that they personally or their organization has not been well-served by computers or technology-assisted learning in the past, they might view e-learning as putting the "cart before the horse." These people think that existing computer systems and computer skills need to be tweaked before venturing into a new area such as e-learning. Heed their advice. It's usually sound. When you identify resistance in your user analysis, it is important to go slowly with implementing e-learning or to develop strategies to prepares people for it.

Work Analysis

Organizations use different approaches to analyze work. The term *work analysis* is used here as an umbrella term to include such needs assessment methods as job study, task analysis, performance analysis, and competency studies. All involve analyzing the job and the required levels of performance. Some look at the ability of individuals or groups to perform at the required levels.

Sample Work Analysis Questions. Use some or all of the sample questions below and consult Table 5.1 to begin an analysis of the information you unearth.

- What work do people perform?
- What standards are people expected to meet while doing the job, especially in terms of the use of technology (hardware and software)?
- Are job incumbents currently meeting these standards, especially in the use of technology?
- For what jobs is e-learning suitable?
- What are the key components of the work being performed?
- What skills and knowledge are required to perform the work?
- What are the different levels of skills and knowledge required within groups or individuals?
- How is successful performance of the work being measured?
- Is individual performance compared to the measures of successful performance?
- Are potential learners performing at the benchmarked levels?
- Where are the gaps?
- What is changing in the work processes, for instance, the introduction of new software?

Collecting data about the work performed and performance problems is particularly important for assessing an organization's readiness for e-learning because it helps to identify areas where e-learning can be used to *enhance performance*. This is the most potent reason why any organization would venture into e-learning in the first place. Your analysis can reveal areas where targeted training can help to make the organization more productive, more efficient, and a less stressful place to work.

If you succeed in giving e-learning a performance orientation, it will not only be easier to justify moving to e-learning, but it will also be easier to evaluate whether the e-learning has brought about the targeted change. In other words, if you know where you are going (in this case, enhanced performance through e-learning), you will be able to tell when you get there (through an evaluation that assesses whether the e-learning delivered the promised performance improvements).

Content Analysis

The purpose of collecting facts about content and analyzing them is to identify what to teach and in what order to teach it. e-Learning materials must flow smoothly and logically. This is particularly essential in self-paced e-learning, where there is no instructor to keep students focused. The data collected during a content analysis helps to establish a logical flow (teaching people to walk before they run). It also helps to ensure that definitions are found for key terms. (Sometimes subject-matter experts wrongly assume that everyone knows key terms.) A content analysis helps designers to chunk the data into digestible morsels (if the material is easy to follow, participants will feel comfortable with it) and ensures that the level and clarity of the content are appropriate to the needs of the users (as established in the user analysis).

Sample Content Analysis Questions. The following are some useful questions for content analysis:

- Are there essential building blocks of knowledge that one needs to learn in order to do the job?
- Are these building blocks of knowledge available in manuals or in other existing documentation?
- In what order and how are these building blocks normally learned?
- What on-the-job documentation is used for teaching?
- Is the existing material available in an electronic format so that it can be converted into instructional materials easily?
- How is this content normally taught?
- What can be done to ensure that the content is taught in a way that makes it seem relevant to the learners?

The "criticality" of any piece of information should be ascertained during a content analysis, and then benchmarks should be established. If it is essential that the users understand the material, it must be included in the training. If it is not critical, it probably does not need to be included. A seasoned performer, sometimes called a subject-matter expert, establishes criticality in concert with the e-learning developer, who may challenge the expert to justify why it is essential to learn particular material.

Training Suitability Analysis

Training is often seen as a quick fix for changing individual and organizational performance but, in reality, the impact of training is limited to providing knowledge, skills, and practice. Now that you have defined performance and content issues, is a learning program the right answer? Will training—in our case, e-learning—have any effect on the performance of the organization in which individuals work? This is the essential question of an e-learning suitability analysis.

Sample Training Suitability Questions. The suggested sample questions below can help you determine whether an e-learning program is going to help resolve a performance issue and whether your solution should focus on training, information, or performance support.

- What are the symptoms of non-performance?
- What are the causes of individual or group non-performance?
- Is non-performance the result of a lack of knowledge, lack of skills, or lack of practice?
- What non-performance is a result of reasons other than a lack of knowledge, skills, or practice?
- What steps will help to bridge the gaps between the standards of performance and the actual performance?
- What solutions can be used to remedy non-performance caused by factors other than a lack of knowledge, skills, or practice?
- Which performance gaps are created by factors that training, knowledge, and performance support cannot address?
- Which performance gaps require solutions such as better management, more discipline, and a referral to support agencies?

Cost/Benefit Analysis

Organizations have the right to demand value from training. A cost/benefit analysis is one method of identifying the value of training. With e-learning, it is even more critical that financial resources not be wasted because e-learning and performance support tools are often expensive to develop.

"Sticker shock" is often cited as one of the factors that makes organizations shy away from recommending technology-assisted learning. However, you should look at all the costs more closely. Despite its typically high front-end costs, e-learning might just turn out to be a bargain. It depends on how many people have to be trained for how long and such factors as their accommodation and travel costs. e-Learning costs have to be compared to the cost of conducting the training in a conventional format.

Sample Cost/Benefit Analysis Questions. To determine whether e-learning is of value, work through the numbers and ask some of the following questions:

- What will it cost to engage everyone involved in all phases of the development and delivery, including learners, leaders, developers, and managers?
- What are the other costs, such as travel and accommodations, equipment, and so on, involved in the development and delivery of the e-learning version of the course?
- What are the other costs, such as travel and accommodations, equipment, and so on, involved in the development and delivery of a similar program in a conventional format?
- What have been the bottom-line benefits of similar programs?
- What benefits of the proposed e-learning program are forecast?
- What will be the return on investment of the proposed e-learning?
- Are there any cost/benefit benchmarks for the proposed e-learning?

The suggested sample questions provide the information you need to start thinking seriously about the costs and benefits of e-learning. However, at this point in your needs identification analysis, you probably do not have all the information about the development of the training that you require to calculate costs accurately.

Before you can accurately forecast the costs of e-learning, you need details about the proposed training design, the training methods, the participants, and other costs. Our list of sample questions covers the essential points for data gathering. There is more information about calculating a cost/benefit analysis ratio, complete with an example, in Chapter Ten of this book.

Additional Information

This seven-step approach has worked for teams that the author has worked with in several different types of organizations. In all cases, the seven areas of questioning were supplemented by a review of internal documentation, Web searches, and interviews with external resources. These three sources provided background information used to tweak the data-gathering strategy. Some cases of the process in action are presented below.

Case 1: Seven-Step Analysis in Action

The client was a public service organization. The team's first task was to map out the data-gathering strategy. We started with a list of questions similar to the sample questions given in this chapter. In a two-hour discussion with the client, we narrowed our list down to twenty questions.

To collect our data from internal resources, we met with fourteen senior stakeholders in individual interviews and twenty-five employees in five focus groups. Interviews took an average of one hour, and focus groups took an average of ninety minutes. We selected questions from the list based on the background of our respondents. We did not use all the questions in each interview. Rather, we found that individuals had pet subjects, and so we explored one to three of the seven areas in each of the fourteen interviews. For example, three of the respondents were closely associated with technology, so we relied on them for our technology analysis. Another respondent had managed the setting up of a professional development center, so we used the meeting with him to learn as much as we could about the users. Another interviewee knew the background details of the project, so we relied on her to provide context data.

Findings from Individual Interviews

From the individual interviews, we learned that there was considerable support for e-learning among senior management. The respondents could see the value of all four types of e-learning and expressed very strong interest in informal learning solutions. They also identified areas where the existing conventional training program had not been fully developed due to a lack of coordination for developing and administering training.

Findings from Focus Groups

Focus groups with operational employees provided different information from the interviews with senior managers, because respondents' backgrounds and experiences were different. The common questions asked in each focus group meeting and the common themes of our findings from the five focus groups follow:

1. What do you (and other people in the organization) need to learn in order to work better?

   The answers included information about laws, cases, and lessons learned doing the work and basic computer skills, such as managing email and using Windows effectively.

2. How do you learn best?

   Focus group members told us that they prefer to learn by doing, although some indicated other styles, too, such as discussing and reading.

3. What has your experience been with computers?

   Some people had obviously done very well with computers and become skilled users. Several mentioned frustration with proprietary software, as it did not contain all the functionality that was promised. And there were problems as well with basic functionality.

4. What has your experience been with training?

   Several participants in the focus groups mentioned that, although there was a program to train instructors, some instructors were only modest communicators.

Force-Field Analysis

We used the data gathered in interviews and focus groups to perform a force-field analysis, using Kurt Lewin's model. This allowed us to identify underlying forces that shaped training and e-learning in the organization. The analysis helped us explain the current situation and show the organization's members what change management steps were needed to help e-learning succeed. It also helped us to point out the risks associated with the intervention and the restraining forces that could impede progress.

We identified eleven restraining forces making it difficult to move ahead with e-learning: heavy workload, limitations of technology, negative technology experiences, one-size-fits-all courses, lag between training and application, uncoordinated approach, unsystematic approach, underutilization of existing materials, lack of instructional skills, resistance to change, and lack of knowledge of existing legislation (shown in Figure 5.1).

FIGURE 5.1. CASE 1: EXAMPLE OF FORCE-FIELD ANALYSIS.

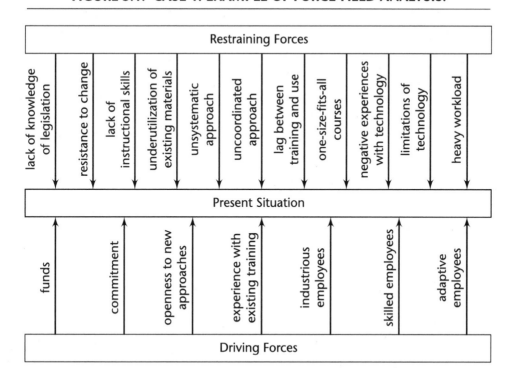

There were seven driving forces propelling the organization toward e-learning: funds, commitment, openness to new approaches, experience with existing training, industrious employees, skilled employees, and adaptive employees (see Figure 5.1).

All of these forces had to be addressed in some way in order to implement e-learning successfully. It was especially important that the eleven restraining forces be lessened. We recommended thirteen steps to move successfully into e-learning. These were aimed at curbing the restraining forces through the creation of training structures, policies, leadership, early wins, evaluation, and recognition to successful users of e-learning.

Results

Based on the data gathered in interviews and focus groups and on our review using a force-field analysis, we recommended the cautious implementation of four types of e-learning:

- Self-paced e-learning in such areas as advanced computer skills
- Leader-led e-learning in such areas as developing soft skills and policies
- Informal learning solutions such as digitized videos of legislation
- Performance support tools for proprietary software

After our recommendations were accepted, we developed prototypes that illustrated the look and feel of the four types of e-learning we had recommended. Once they were approved and tweaked, we helped the organization move gradually into its e-learning program.

Case 2: Simple Force-Field Analysis

This case illustrates a simplified approach to assessing whether an organization is ready for e-learning. In a half-day meeting with a manufacturing corporation, we addressed one question: what has been the experience to date with technology-assisted learning?

I [the author] wrote replies on 8 1/2 by 11 inch sheets of paper, divided lengthwise and taped to a wall with masking tape. On the top half of the wall, I affixed the experiences that participants told me would restrain the organization from implementing e-learning; on the bottom half, I wrote the forces they said would help to drive the organization to e-learning. In a second phase, in the comfort of my office, I grouped the forces into categories and prepared a force-field diagram (Figure 5.2).

Driving Forces

The driving forces for implementing e-learning in this organization were grouped into five categories: experience, framework, planning, support, and technology.

Experience

- Several business units are on-board with training
- Some e-learning has been successfully used
- The first catalog of courses has been produced
- e-Learning has been shown to reduce training costs in our organization

Framework

- e-Learning will allow business units to track training usage
- e-Learning would be a way to distribute information from the best practices teams
- e-Learning fosters systematic learning against business goals as captured on competency statements

Planning

- Leadership is considering setting up learning resource centers
- Some departments have topics they would like to see taught via e-learning
- There is a plan to conduct a company-wide needs assessment of training needs

Support

- Existing libraries of CD-ROMs
- Greater participation in training will be a way to increase the level of satisfaction with training

Technology

- Intranet is running

Restraining Forces

The categories of restraining forces were the same except that there were no observations in the category of support.

Experience

- Business units do not use a consistent process to report training
- Employees and supervisors do not have experience planning training and linking it to career development
- Libraries of CD-ROMs exist, but their utilization is unknown

Framework

- Inconsistent trainer skills and inconsistent availability of support
- Lack of a common culture
- Lack of a learning organization

Planning

- Lack of career planning

Technology

- Intranet is up, but not everyone has access
- IT is not resourced to provide an adequate level of support

Lessons Learned

Experience with the approaches described in this chapter have yielded important lessons about how to determine whether e-learning is appropriate for a particular organization. Some of the lessons and their implications for assessing organizational readiness for e-learning are

- *Keep an open mind.* It is surprising how much high-quality input you can obtain from people in focus groups and interviews when you approach them with an open mind. *Implications:* Open-minded consultation will generate rich input. People you consult with will have plenty to say, so your time must be carefully managed.
- *Use several methods of data collection.* The different methods help to generate different data. *Implications:* It is possible to use several methods of data collection to yield worthwhile results. For example, a questionnaire will generate solid data about users of e-learning, whereas a focus group meeting with the same people will unveil their attitudes.

FIGURE 5.2. CASE 2: DRIVING AND RESTRAINING FORCES IMPACTING E-LEARNING.

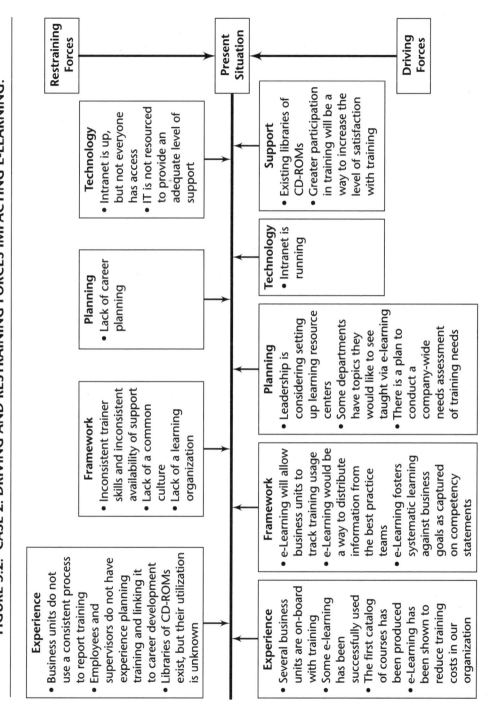

Restraining Forces

Experience
- Business units do not use a consistent process to report training
- Employees and supervisors do not have experience planning training and linking it to career development
- Libraries of CD-ROMs exist, but their utilization is unknown

Framework
- Inconsistent trainer skills and inconsistent availability of support
- Lack of a common culture
- Lack of a learning organization

Planning
- Lack of career planning

Technology
- Intranet is up, but not everyone has access
- IT is not resourced to provide an adequate level of support

Present Situation

Experience
- Several business units are on-board with training
- Some e-learning has been successfully used
- The first catalog of courses has been produced
- e-Learning has been shown to reduce training costs in our organization

Framework
- e-Learning will allow business units to track training usage
- e-Learning would be a way to distribute information from the best practice teams
- e-Learning fosters systematic learning against business goals as captured on competency statements

Planning
- Leadership is considering setting up learning resource centers
- Some departments have topics they would like to see taught via e-learning
- There is a plan to conduct a company-wide needs assessment of training needs

Technology
- Intranet is running

Support
- Existing libraries of CD-ROMs
- Greater participation in training will be a way to increase the level of satisfaction with training

Driving Forces

- *Be aware of the organizational climate for data collection.* Selecting the right methods for collecting e-learning data is an important issue for organizations. *Implications:* If you make the right choice in a given organization, you'll get solid information. The right choice in one organization could be the wrong one in another.
- *Consider varying your approach with large populations.* If you have a large population to interview, it may be best to use different approaches for different segments. *Implications:* For example, interviewees who are close at hand can be gathered into focus groups. Senior stakeholders might appreciate short, individual interviews. An email questionnaire could be sent to people who are geographically dispersed, but telephone calls would be better if your target audience receives a large number of email messages and has trouble finding the time to answer email.
- *Whatever methods you select, craft your questions carefully. Implications:* When respondents misinterpret a question or have trouble understanding it, they can become sidetracked. Check your questions with people who have finely honed judgment and test the questions with members of the target group.

Even the comprehensive methodology for gathering data explained here is not the most rigorous methodology. Although more than fifty questions that you can ask were presented here, we invite you to think critically about them and use only the ones that you deem necessary in your situation. Plan your questioning strategy carefully. Write the questions in advance. Show them to a trusted friend or colleague and ask for feedback. Tweak. Practice. Test. Share your questions and overall approach with stakeholders and ask for feedback before you start your questioning. Get buy-in. Send the questions to busy interviewees in advance. They will appreciate the opportunity to formulate their answers in advance, and even though they might not find the time to answer every question in detail, you are likely to receive richer data than you would have by asking your questions point-blank.

Test Drive

Spending a few minutes filling in the chart that follows will help you better understand the concepts and models discussed here.

First, select an organization. It does not have to have an extensive e-learning program now, but it should be at least a candidate for e-learning. Be easy on yourself; don't use a situation that is unusually complex by virtue of size or diversity. Next, using the seven areas of analysis, identify the "facts" in the situation you chose. (You may conduct interviews if you wish, but they are not necessary for this exercise. This time, we invite you to guess the facts or to convey them as you see them from your limited knowledge.)

Topic	Facts
1. Context	
2. Technology	
3. Users	
4. Work	
5. Content	
6. Training suitability	
7. Cost/benefit	

From the facts you listed above, select the driving forces and restraining forces that influence the movement toward e-learning in the organization.

Driving Forces	**Restraining Forces**

Explain your findings to someone who knows the situation. Ask for his or her feedback about the quality of your analysis, the accuracy of your data, and the usefulness of the force-field analysis.

CHAPTER SIX

SPOTLIGHT ON LEARNING

Frameworks for Design and Development

Undoubtedly you have experienced the excitement that a talented instructor can spark in a room of participants. You listen intently. You consider each point. Engagement. Learning. Long-term application. These are the results of effective classroom instruction. They are also what we need to strive for in e-learning.

The term *e-learning* puts the emphasis where it should be—on learning. e-Learning connotes *outputs*—the acquisition of skills, knowledge, and attitudes. The terms *training* and *teaching*, on the other hand, emphasize techniques for delivering the message—*inputs*. While inputs are important to the success of learning, they are only part of the story. Instructional designers should concentrate on outputs such as measured increases in job and business performance, either in the quality of goods and services produced or in the job satisfaction of employees producing those goods and services. Solid instruction is concentrated on what people need to learn to enhance their performance as students or workers. A better understanding of what constitutes successful learning and how to achieve it helps managers with the selection of courseware from vendors and helps instructional designers in the creation of materials.

> "When I started to develop e-learning, I had no help. So it was difficult at first. I wish I had taken the time to learn about all the resources that exist."
> —Allan, e-learning course leader

This chapter outlines three frameworks for learning design and delivery that e-learning instructors, developers, and managers often look to in program development. Whether you are developing programs and courses from scratch or purchasing off the shelf, these models can be used to guide your decisions on the direction and shape your e-learning program will take. Besides the broad implications, we also spotlight design and development techniques that can help make the e-learner's experience a successful one.

But first, a basic understanding of what we mean by "learning."

What Is Learning?

Most training professionals will recognize at least six types of learning, ranging from knowledge (the least complex) to evaluation (the most complex). These six types of learning are achieved in different ways, and they require different learning strategies (see Table 6.1).

Learners must first acquire the lower level skills (knowledge, comprehension, and application, for example) before they can perform the higher level skills (analysis, synthesis, and evaluation). The different levels are also taught differently. The higher level skills require carefully designed application exercises to ensure that the learning has occurred and has "stuck." For example, if the focus is on learning to synthesize the concepts of e-learning as presented in this book, an effective learning program would ensure that participants acquired the basic knowledge of the four types of e-learning, were able to explain them either orally or in writing, could explain the relationships between e-learning and conventional learning, and would be able to synthesize or use this knowledge in a specific situation to recommend what types of e-learning to use.

> "Designers often fall into the trap of referring to 'the learner' as if there is one learner—or that all learners are clones of the same learner. Such thinking can lead you to oversimplify your approach by assuming that all learners are alike. Not only are learners rarely the same, [but] they vary in their attitudes and abilities from hour to hour and even minute to minute."[1]   —William Horton, *Instructional Design for Online Learning*, from www.macromedia.com/learning, p. 21.

TABLE 6.1. SIX TYPES OF LEARNING.*

Type of Learning	Description	Example
1. Knowledge	Recall of facts, methods, and concepts	Name the five steps in a process
2. Comprehension	Explain or summarize material	Describe how employees use the process
3. Application	Use rules and concepts in new situations	Use the process to perform a work-related task
4. Analysis	Determine the relationships between parts of a system	Identify overlap in the phases of the process
5. Synthesis	Form new patterns or structures	Redesign the process
6. Evaluation	Judge the value of content	Compare the process to others

*Source: Canadian Forces Individual Training and Education

Learning Styles and e-Learning

Understanding and succeeding with e-learning starts with understanding learning in general. A first step to understanding learning in general is an understanding of learning styles. People have ways they prefer to learn, which are often called *preferred* learning styles. The most effective teaching methods, whether in the classroom or through a computer, are those that accommodate the preferred learning styles of the people being taught.

There are many schools of thought about learning styles, but no universally accepted approach to defining them or adjusting instructional designs and methods to account for them. Nor does everyone agree on their significance. One of the easier to grasp and most widely used approaches is from David Kolb.[2] He has written extensively about four types of learners, described as: divergers, assimilators, accommodators, and convergers. According to Kolb:

- *Convergers* perceive information *abstractly* and process it *reflectively*. They learn by sequential thinking and are attentive to detail. The emphasis for convergers is to think rationally and concretely while remaining relatively unemotional.

- *Divergers* acquire knowledge through *intuition*. Individuals with this preferred style of learning draw on their imaginative aptitude and their ability to view complex situations from many perspectives. Divergers' imaginative ability is their greatest strength.
- *Assimilators* create theoretical models and reason *inductively*. Assimilators learn by thinking and analyzing and then planning and reflecting. Assimilators focus on the development of *theories*.
- *Accommodators* are dynamic learners who relish change, risk taking, and flexibility. Accomodators' greatest strengths are their ability for *getting things done* and for *becoming fully involved* in new experiences. They approach problems in an intuitive, trial-and-error manner. They obtain information from other people rather than through their own analytical abilities.

Designers of e-learning must consider the different learning styles. First, it is critical to identify the predominant learning styles of the people who will be taking the e-learning program. Research indicates, for example, that recent graduates from high school prefer concrete action.[3] The same research indicates that instructors tend to prefer an abstract approach to learning.

In other words, young people prefer to learn by doing, while instructors prefer to learn by developing concepts. Potential trouble here! At least there could be trouble if instructors teach youth in the way that they personally prefer to learn. (We sometimes do this.) Developers of e-learning materials must also take care to ensure that their own preferred learning styles do not govern the instructional design. (This is a real risk.) Instead, the developer must consider the learning styles of the people who will be taking the e-learning program—and they could be convergers, divergers, assimilators, or accommodators, or likely a mix of all four. Table 6.2 gives examples of effective e-learning activities for Kolb's four learning styles.

Several questionnaires have been developed to identify learning styles. Many are available commercially. Others are available free on the Web. You can locate the current commercial and free questionnaires by conducting Web searches on phrases such as "preferred learning styles" and "learning style questionnaire."

TABLE 6.2. E-LEARNING ACTIVITIES FOR KOLB'S LEARNING STYLES.

Learning Style	Preferences	Examples of Effective e-Learning Activities
Convergers	Think rationally and concretely	Developing a point of view from online documentation or observation defending the point of view.
Divergers	Intuitive	Participating in a role play and assuming the persona of those with a particular point of view.
Assimilators	Development of theories	Searching the Web to find materials illustrating different points of view about the same topic. Analyzing these points of view and explaining them. Participating in a discussion among participants about a controversial topic.
Accommodators	Becoming fully involved in new experiences	Searching for materials on the Web. Posting questions to a community of practice, obtaining information, and engaging respondents to the posting.

A word of caution: learning styles are not cast in concrete. Learners are not always hooked on one style. Mel Silberman (author of the foreword to this book), a professor at Temple University and leading author about training, says that, in every group of thirty participants, an average of twenty-two are able to learn effectively as long as an instructor provides a blend of visual, auditory, and kinesthetic activities.[4] Silberman concludes that the most effective approach to teaching caters to a variety of learning styles.

Gagné on Learning

Robert Gagné's learning model is another solid framework for developing and delivering e-learning. It depicts nine "events" that need to be included in an effective learning sequence:

1. Gain attention.
2. Inform learners of objectives.
3. Stimulate recall of prior learning.
4. Present the content.

5. Provide learning guidance.

6. Elicit performance (practice).

7. Provide feedback.

8. Assess performance.

9. Enhance retention and transfer to the job.

You will no doubt recognize these steps as what good classroom presenters do. However, had you thought of including them in e-learning? Think about it. Don't you agree that self-paced and leader-led e-learning would be more compelling if the design included these nine steps?

Take a look at Table 6.3 to see how the Gagné model can help to create effective learning in both conventional and e-learning situations.

TABLE 6.3. GAGNÉ'S MODEL APPLIED TO E-LEARNING.

Events	Purpose	Techniques	Informal	Self-Paced	Leader-Led	Performance Support
1. Gain attention	Starts the learning process	Engaging questions, engaging graphics and sound effects, interesting facts	X	X	X	
2. Inform learners of objectives	Helps learners to set expectations for the e-learning materials	State objectives, explain what will and will not be covered. In leader-led, engage learners in a discussion about the objectives		X	X	
3. Stimulate recall of prior learning	Helps learners to compare new information to what they know and to associate the new information with the old information in long-term memory	Questions about the meaning of words, questions about previous experiences, questions about key concepts in the session; discussion about participants' knowledge of the subject		X	X	

Events	Purpose	Techniques	Informal	Self-Paced	Leader-Led	Performance Support
4. Present the content	Conveys the new knowledge	Present in a logical order; present in short segments; use a variety of media; use self-paced e-learning	X	X	X	X
5. Provide learning guidance	Helps to move information into long-term memory	Use examples, memorable graphics, and mnemonics	X	X	X	X
6. Elicit performance (practice)	Helps learners confirm their understanding	Learners practice the skills, use new knowledge, or apply to their situation		X	X	X
7. Provide feedback	Helps learners to know whether they have absorbed the new knowledge and skills	Feedback should be immediate and specific from the instructor or from fellow participants		X	X	
8. Assess performance	Helps learners to realize whether they have mastered the subject	A comprehensive performance test that could involve several teaching points		X	X	X
9. Enhance retention and transfer to the job	Helps to ensure that training is judged to be successful	Job aids, templates, performance tools, as well as discussions about experiences and lessons learned	X	X	X	X

Five Stages of e-Learning

A third framework for e-learning design and development comes from Gilly Salmon, an e-learning thought leader from the U.K.'s Open University, who has been involved in e-learning for some fifteen years.[5] She suggests that one must plan for five stages in e-learning (her term is *"computer medi-ated conferencing"*):

1. Access and motivation,
2. Online socialization,
3. Information exchange,
4. Knowledge construction,
5. Development.

FIGURE 6.1. SALMON'S FIVE-PHASE MODEL FOR ONLINE LEARNING.

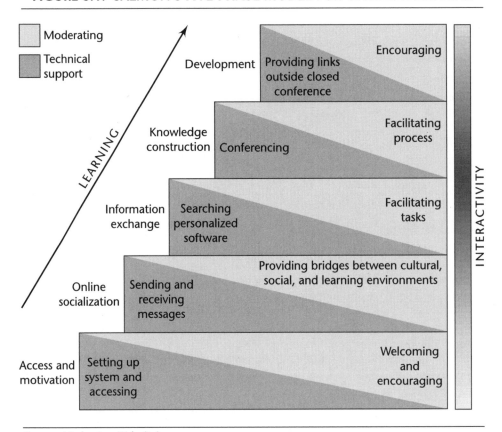

Source: eModerators Web site[6]

Salmon sees two types of actions that students and instructors undertake in each of the five phases: technical and instructional (see Figure 6.1). Her emphasis on technical support helps instructors to acknowledge this important area also. There is a tendency among instructors to distance themselves from technical issues. However, such issues can undermine e-learning, and instructors must monitor them and work to ensure that they are addressed. It's not good enough to say that the techies messed up! *A good online instructor finds solutions for technical problems—or finds someone with the solution.*

Table 6.4 gives some examples of technical and instructional actions that developers and instructors might consider for each of Salmon's five phases. There is also a step-by-step portrayal of the model from the perspectives of both learner and instructor in Chapter Eight.

TABLE 6.4. DESIGN AND DELIVERY IMPLICATIONS
           OF THE SALMON MODEL.

Stage	Technical Actions	Instructional Actions
1. Access and motivation	Setting up system and accessing (working with technical experts)	Welcoming and encouraging (a warm, explicit welcome that motivates and orients learners)
2. Online socialization	Sending and receiving messages (using a threaded discussion, chat, or both)	Providing bridges between people and perceptions (exercises to help people get to know one another)
3. Information exchange	Searching, personalizing software (helping students understand and use software features)	Facilitating tasks and supporting use of learning materials (facilitating discussions by providing information to students, receiving their input, and providing feedback)
4. Knowledge construction	Conferencing (using software such as threaded discussion, chat, and streaming video)	Facilitating process (encouraging group work and replies to postings, establishing standards for postings)
5. Development	Providing links outside the closed conferences (students explore beyond the actual discussion and discover on their own)	Encouraging (supporting students' individual activities, responding to their specific questions)

Source: e-Moderating: The Key to Teaching and Learning Online, by Gilly Salmon

Engaging the Learner to Make Learning Stick

> "As with most things we take for granted, courses have been around for so long we accept that they have well-known characteristics that don't change and leave it at that. Nothing could be further from the truth. We remember little of what we hear in a classroom because it is not easy to listen when someone talks. To really connect with what lecturers say requires us to stop listening and think. Often we think about something else entirely. Professors know this, which is why there are tests."[7]
> —Dr. Roger Schank, director of the Institute for the Learning Sciences (ILS) at Northwestern University and a leader in the field of artificial intelligence and multimedia-based interactive training

It's important to base your decisions for the design and delivery of e-learning on solid models such as Gagné's, Salmon's, and the challenges of Schank; however, in order to make learning stick, you must go further and incorporate into your e-learning design interactive learning techniques. You must address "What's in it for me?" You have to nurture the learner-instructor relationship. It is easy to imagine such elements being part of leader-led e-learning, but they can also be part of self-paced, informal learning, and electronic support tools.

Interactive Learning

Much has been written about the virtue of interactive learning—using questions, exercises, and other activities to engage learners as active participants in the learning process. Interactive learning keeps students energized and helps participants absorb information and remember it. Why? How?

First, interactive learning helps students focus. To understand how this works, consider that the human brain functions five or six times faster than instructors speak or e-learning audio files play. If a classroom instructor, an online instructor, or an e-learning module limits the messages to facts, participants whose minds are working five times as fast as the information is being delivered will start to draw their own conclusions—and perhaps daydream about subjects not related to the material being taught.

Clearly, interaction is a valuable component of a successful learning experience. But how to create interaction in e-learning? As an instructor, instructional designer, or administrator, you must think clearly about interactivity.

Clicking on a hyperlink is a mild form of interaction, but hyperlinks are not known to ask a question back, to challenge your ideas, to force you to consider your ideas further. Carefully designed learning activities challenge learners, even in a self-directed format. From the classroom, we have learned much about the benefits of active learning. What we learned in the classroom can he applied to e-learning. Games are one engaging activity from the classroom that can be applied to e-learning, and there are several others.

> "Passive learning alone doesn't engage our higher brain functions or stimulate our senses to the point where we integrate our lessons into our existing schemes. We must do something with our knowledge."[8]
>
> —Marcia Conner

Questions and Answers

When an instructor of an e-learning package asks learners what a topic or a word means to them, they start to draw from their personal experiences. If, for example, an instructor asks you what CBT means, images start to appear in your mind's eye of CBT programs you have used. Or if you have never used CBT, what you've heard about it comes to mind. You are linking the questions to your experience. You are finding the relevance in the topic—for you. You are interacting. Your mind is linking information and learning. In the same way, "why" questions engage learners. Questions such a "Why is this important?" invite listeners to think about the reasons for studying something. Once learners, especially adult learners, see the reason for learning about a topic, they focus more clearly. They soak up information much better.

Learners remember more when instructors—and e-learning modules—use interactive learning methods. The human brain remembers what it processes. Asking questions, discussing, and using information in other ways helps people to retain it. Do you learn better when an instructor or self-paced materials ask questions? Do questions engage you? Sometimes questions can be more important than answers. Do you agree? If you don't, I suggest that you sign up for an e-learning course over the Web. I hope the topic will be terrific or you will have an engaging instructor who poses plenty of thought-provoking questions, because if you don't you might become another drop-out statistic. Walking in the shoes of a learner puts things in perspective.

However, simply asking questions is not enough. Instructional designers and instructors must ensure that students participate in answering the questions. e-Learning is ideal for fostering participative questioning, with opportunities to ask and answer questions through chat, bulletin boards, listservs, and videoconferencing. Threaded discussions, bulletin boards, and listservs are ideal for learners who like to mull over their replies, because they can read a question one day, think about an answer the next, and reply whenever they wish.

Playing with e-Learning

"You can export almost anything you can do in the form of a classroom game to an online, Web-based activity," says Dr. Sivasailam "Thiagi" Thiagarajan, president of Workshops by Thiagi and the premier spokesperson for games and fun in learning. "The secret lies in your deciding whether some of the classroom activities are worth conducting in the first place. And the greatest secret involves your identifying unique characteristics of the e-learning environment (speed, graphics, mathematical modeling, multimedia, automatic data trapping, adjustment to the player's flow level) and exploiting them in the design of your games."[9]

Brainstorming, case studies, and guided research are just a few of the successful techniques from our classroom experience that you can adapt to e-learning. Examples of how they might be used are shown in Table 6.5. They can be adapted to work with any subject matter and any size of group.

TABLE 6.5. ADAPTING CLASSROOM METHODS TO E-LEARNING.

Activity	Learners	Using the Activity in e-Learning
Brainstorming	Present a large number of ideas about a topic without criticism	To gather many thoughts or opinions on a topic

Activity	Learners	Using the Activity in e-Learning
Case studies	Study a written summary of an event or events to discuss and draw conclusions	To teach complex knowledge
Drill and practice	Practice applying specific knowledge or a well-defined skill	To help learners memorize facts or to test their knowledge
Game	Learn through simulation	To give learners a memorable experience in performing a task without the risk or cost of the real activity
Group project	Work in groups to produce a group output	To develop deep knowledge and skills through having to explain ideas and debate issues
Guided research	Collect, analyze, and report on research	To help learners discover resources on the Web and to develop their analysis skills
Hands-on activity	Perform a real task	To teach skills and to help learners transfer knowledge through practice
Scavenger hunt	Find information on the Internet or on their corporate intranet	To develop Web research skills
Scenario	Adopt assigned roles in simulations	To develop deep knowledge and skills
Seminar	Present their ideas and receive comments from other participants and the instructor	To develop in-depth knowledge and the ability to articulate thoughts about a specific subject
Virtual laboratory	Conduct experiments online using simulators	To learn to operate real laboratory equipment
Webcast	View a digitized video on a computer monitor	To convey large amounts of information to learners

What's in It for Me? (WIIFM)

WIIFM is like a radio station that people frequently tune into. Whether it's conventional training or e-learning, we adults look to learning for the benefits that it will bestow. Will the learning make us happier, wealthier, wiser—or more competent in our work? e-Learning can address the WIIFM motivation phenomenon by including clear explanations of what a learner stands to gain from the learning materials. What are the benefits of the learning? How can the new skills and knowledge be used? How have they been used by others? Behavioral learning objectives that inform participants what they will be able to do after they have completed a learning event are examples of using WIIFM. One example would be "At the end of the session, participants will be able to name four types of e-learning and apply the types to a case study." Another example of using WIIFM occurs when an instructor or an e-learning module asks a learner to identify what he or she is looking for in a learning experience. Simply asking learners why they are enrolled in a learning experience can help to identify WIIFM.

Nurturing and e-Learning

It is a truism about humans that we perform best when others nurture us—when others acknowledge us and provide positive feedback. An interactive instructional framework creates a rich environment for nurturing. The questions of interactive online instruction (both leader-led and self-paced), when posed in a caring, respectful way, establish a meaningful relationship between participants and instructors. Through online discussion and group work, e-learning achieves a high-level of nurturing, and this in turn fosters learning.

Another commonly quoted "fact" is that humans convey more messages by their nonverbal behavior (what they do) than by their verbal behavior (what they say). Some authors suggest that over 90 percent of communication occurs at the nonverbal level.[10] Common sense might suggest that this figure is inflated. Nevertheless, you probably agree that nonverbal behavior is an important factor in conveying messages, and there is little doubt that interactive classroom instruction, with its emphasis on eye contact, listening, and nurturing, involves people, engages them, and encourages learning. We have had a few millennia to learn to engage people face-to-face in classroom-like situations, but how can we do it online? Certainly it is a challenge. However, if you talk to successful online learners and instructors, they will tell you it can be done. Online or "virtual" communities are very real. They foster meaningful discussion and build a sense of camaraderie.

Building Online Communities

In a classroom, an instructor helps to build a sense of community by asking questions, by modeling behavior, and by setting up and encouraging cooperative group work. An online instructor, in either a synchronous or an asynchronous mode, also asks questions, models participative behavior, and sets up and encourages cooperative group work. Online instructors find that this process can take more time online than it does in the classroom, as they must respond individually to every participant's online messages. Responding means keyboarding a reply, which inevitably takes more time than giving an oral reply.

Online instructors need to find ways to move themselves out of the spotlight and into the background. One way to do this is to have the entire group of participants take on some of the community-building activities. Some instructors extricate themselves from some or most of the discussion by having subgroups of participants meet to discuss issues. The instructors monitor the discussion and intervene as required.

Other Design and Development Issues

Synchronous Versus Asynchronous

One of the big issues in e-learning development is whether it is delivered in a synchronous or in an asynchronous mode. *Synchronous* e-learning parallels live classroom learning. Learners and instructors are communicating in real time. (Generally this means simultaneously, but some people insist that it is synchronous even if there are delays of hours.) Synchronous learning has the advantage of conveying the same information to everyone at the same time. A potential use of synchronous e-learning would be when a senior manager wishes to make a presentation to a large number of people. By using webcast technology, the presentation could be delivered in a synchronous mode to employees who have access to a browser and to the company network. It could also be saved at a Web site and viewed later by employees who were not able to view the original presentation. In the first instance, the video would be an example of a live, synchronous presentation. In the second instance, it would be an example of delayed asynchronous e-learning.

Asynchronous e-learning clearly separates learners and instructors in time. It parallels email. Learners send messages to instructors and the instructors reply later, when they are available. Asynchronous learning has the advantage of allowing learners and instructors to reflect on questions and answers that are posted to a discussion area, sometimes called a bulletin board, and to reply when ready.

How do we decide which one to use? Your choice of technologies is influenced by who, what, when, how, and how many. Table 6.6 illustrates factors to consider in making your decision about whether to use synchronous or asynchronous approaches to e-learning.

Like most topics in this book, making choices between synchronous and asynchronous learning is not an either-or situation. They can be combined. Many courses warm up participants with asynchronous activities and use synchronous discussions after the die is cast. Other instructors have had good results by starting with a synchronous activity and later using asynchronous. Table 6.6 equates asynchronous e-learning with threaded discussions and synchronous e-learning with online chat. Synchronous also refers to online video. You will find that several of the considerations for online chat are the same as for online video.

TABLE 6.6. FACTORS TO CONSIDER WHEN CHOOSING SYNCHRONOUS OR ASYNCHRONOUS MEANS.

Criterion	Question	Synchronous (Chat)	Asynchronous
Who	Learners' level of autonomy	Learners are not autonomous and require a scheduled program to keep them engaged	Learners are autonomous
Who	Learners' typing ability	If learners type well	If learners do not type well
What	Learners need to learn	Learners have the same or very similar needs	Learners have diverse needs
When	Learners are available	At same time	At various times
Where	Learners are located	Located in close or same time zones	Located in diverse time zones

Criterion	Question	Synchronous	Asynchronous
How	Learners prefer to learn or instructors prefers to instruct	Experts online or discussion with fellow students in chat sessions	Discovering new information and progressing at their own pace
How many	Number of learners	Small number using chat	Larger numbers

Behavioral Theory and e-Learning

Approaches to learning advocated by behavioral psychologists have shaped the way that many present-day e-learning programs are designed and conducted. Behaviorists such as Skinner, Guthrie, and Hull[11] advocate breaking learning into small components and teaching in small segments with plenty of feedback. This approach is evident in the task-analysis approach to designing training, where an instructional designer breaks work into task, duties, and activities.

Training modules are next built to help learners perform tasks. The modules are taught one at a time, ideally with feedback between modules.

In the extreme behaviorist view, a teaching machine could be used to instruct and provide feedback when answers are right. B.F. Skinner led the quest[12] for a teaching machine in the 1960s, and one of the offshoots was text-based programmed instruction. The programmed instruction manuals were simple devices to present small amounts of information in frames. Learners responded to questions and were given feedback according to the answers they provided. This same approach of information, question, response, and feedback was embedded in early versions of computer-based training.

With the popularity of CD-ROM technology in the early 1990s, self-study took on a new life. What had been dull, wordy computer-based training was replaced by multimedia. Combining images, voice, and videos now makes self-study more engaging, more entertaining.

The Case Against Pizzazz

One of the issues that CBT multimedia—and now e-learning—faces is how to design materials so that instruction is emphasized, rather than pizzazz. In the case of the first CBT programs, some did effectively instruct, through presentations, application, and feedback. But others simply put information on a monitor and hoped for the best. The interaction of "learners" was sometimes limited to reading text on a screen and selecting a button on the screen to advance to the next page. CBT programs like these were sometimes derisively called electronic page turners. (Putting similar listless materials on the Web gives birth to a new derogatory term: html page turners.)

Even with color, sound, graphics, and video added, electronic (or html) page turners are still page turners. Also, the addition of menus and the accompanying opportunities to select content does not make a page turner into a successful instructional device. A thoughtful instructional strategy is needed to reap the benefits of technology-assisted learning and to avoid the pitfalls of mindless pizzazz and information overload.

Facilitating the Process

The common thread through all the models and methods presented in this chapter is that instructors and designers must facilitate the process of learning. There is nothing new there, but with e-learning we need to pay even more attention to our instructional and developmental skills.

This is because, once designed, e-learning is less flexible. In conventional learning, instructors have opportunities to modify training materials in response to student questions and other events that occur in the classroom. There is less opportunity for on-the-fly revisions of e-learning materials. In many leader-led courses, especially asynchronous ones, instructors tend to post all course materials to the course Web site before the course begins and students have the opportunity to look ahead at materials. Therefore it would confuse students if many revisions were made after the course started. With self-paced e-learning, there are even fewer opportunities to make on-the-fly changes because the training is distributed via canned presentations, whether on CD-ROM or over the Web.

e-Learning developers need to keep working at crafting course designs that help them facilitate learning. Instructors need to be able to step outside of ongoing activities, assess the individual online discussion and course processes, and, if necessary, take steps to make improvements. Understanding and using the *nine steps* and *five stages* helps instructors and developers assess and revise their materials and their roles.

A Final Thought

By way of summary, Figure 6.2 depicts key attributes of successful e-learning. The diagram summarizes four key attributes: learning professionals, learners, content, and technology. As you bring e-learning into your organization, your goal should be to match the qualities of a successful learning experience by using the criteria pictured or by using others that your organization sets. Are your learning professionals, learners, content, and technology up to the task? Any one criteria can undermine your success. Some classroom learning events miss the mark. It's the same with e-learning; not all e-learning is created equal. Taking a reasoned approach to e-learning will help you succeed. You need to understand learning, apply this understanding to e-learning, get past the myths or hype, and find reality. You can help to ensure that learning sticks by using simple approaches to design and delivery that are based on solid models and proven methods such as the ones we offer here and throughout the book.

FIGURE 6.2. KEY ATTRIBUTES OF SUCCESSFUL E-LEARNING.

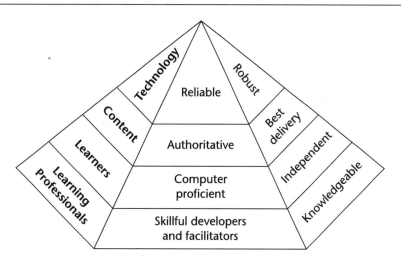

Test Drive

Everyone reading this book shares common learning experiences. Readers have participated in structured learning—most likely formal schooling and probably training courses designed to teach you to do your job better. What criteria have you used in the past to say that an educational or training event was good or bad? What helps you to learn? Think about a rich learning experience you have had in the past. What made the experience successful? Compare your thoughts with the ideas presented in Figure 6.3.

Learners, instructors, developers, and administrators all select different attributes of a successful learning event. The e-learning challenge is to find ways to ensure that e-learning offers what all four groups require. Can e-learning match leader-led learning for interactivity and nurturing? As it stands now, e-learning probably cannot match all aspects of leader-led learning. An excellent classroom instructor has an advantage over an excellent online instructor, simply because face-to-face interaction is more dynamic. But an excellent online discussion is probably equivalent to what a good instructor can do in the classroom.

Undoubtedly, e-learning can be an effective instructional approach for your organization. This book will help you excel at e-learning by discovering the right way to select, develop, and administer e-learning—for you personally and for the people you serve. But keep this in mind: it does not need to be an either-or situation. e-Learning does not have to replace classroom programs. In some cases, you can combine the two, gaining the benefits of both.

FIGURE 6.3. QUALITIES OF A SUCCESSFUL LEARNING EXPERIENCE.

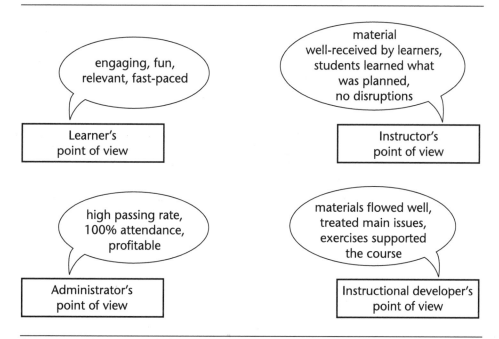

Source: An email message to the author on January 16, 2001.

CHAPTER SEVEN

DECISION MAKING STEP BY STEP

Selecting Courses and Vendors*

Transitioning to e-learning can consume large amounts of resources: financial and time. One of the major decisions organizations have to make is selecting which training to deliver in an e-learning mode. When they make the right decision, they save both time and money. This chapter presents a framework for making solid decisions about which training to deliver in an e-learning mode. We have also included a decision-making model and assessment tools for selecting e-learning courseware and vendors.

A Question of Priorities

Selecting training to deliver in an e-learning mode is fundamentally about setting priorities. The underlying questions are important and complex. How do you decide priorities? What processes ensure that you set the right

*We are grateful to Elizabeth Syversten-Bitten and Peter Sabiston for providing their research papers on the topics covered in this chapter. Yvon Côté and Dan Hansen also made substantial contributions to this chapter. For further information on this topic, see *Quality Standards for Evaluating Multimedia and Online Training,* by Lynette Gillis, McGraw-Hill, 2000.

priorities? Who decides in the end? Will a systematic process be followed, or will senior management make the final decision without considering the findings of the exercise? The stakes can be high. Setting the right priorities helps to ensure success.

The questions in the process of selecting e-learning courses and materials are also complex. Should an organization select the course that will reach the largest number of people? Is the best course one that targets skill shortages? Do you target courses that will save the most in travel costs? Should e-learning courses be very closely job-related or should they be of general interest? Is the best candidate a course with content that does not change? Alternatively, is the best course one that changes frequently? Moreover, how does the commitment to training that is *any time, anywhere,* and perhaps *for anyone* fit into the e-learning model and the selection of courseware? Should an organization develop its own e-learning materials, purchase from an outside vendor, or subscribe to courses offered by a service provider? Or are there opportunities to partner with other organizations, associations, schools—or even your competition—in developing e-learning?

The framework presented here represents priority setting as a standardized, linear, logical process. It is not. Priority setting is ultimately intuitive and dependent on the judgment of the people involved. Priority setting is also a product of the context on the day when the priorities are set. In a hierarchical organization, priorities may be heavily influenced by the thinking or whims of its leaders. Nevertheless, facts, numbers, and experience play a role in the decision-making process. Or at least they should. So the approach described in this chapter is not a prescribed standard. It is a framework for better understanding a process and for approaching a difficult situation with a degree of calmness and critical thinking.

A priority setting process can help decide both short-term and long-term approaches to e-learning. For example, in some cases there will be an immediate decision to deliver e-learning about a specific topic. In another situation, the conclusion could be that there are insufficient funds to take the recommended action. If so, the data gathered in the process can be used to build a business case.

Building Blocks

There are four main ways to build an inventory of e-learning materials. They can be leased, purchased, converted, or built from the ground up. There are several possible approaches. Many organizations subscribe to learning events through a service provider or an application service provider (ASP). Some organizations decide to purchase e-learning materials, such as self-paced courses about software bundled on CD-ROM or distributed over the Web. Other groups convert existing instructor-led workshops to leader-led online courses, while others build their e-learning materials from scratch.

With the process we recommend for selecting training courses to deliver as e-learning, the resulting courseware could be leased, purchased, converted, or built from scratch. Either internal staff or external resources can lead the processes described here. Whatever approach you take, hard work and rigorous thinking remain the principal ingredients for selecting training courses to deliver as e-learning.

Making the Decision, Step by Step

Whatever approach you take, you must decide which courses to tackle first. You probably don't have the financial and human resources to launch your organization into a wall-to-wall e-learning system, so you will need a decision-making process to help you decide where to start. Figure 7.1 provides such a process. It's an elaborate one, most suitable for a large organization, but you can scale it down to meet the needs of your particular group. It will help you decide which courses to broach first. Used judiciously, the process can help you make sound and successful decisions. The process is explained fully in the following text.

1. Create the Selection Process

Creating the selection process means determining who will lead the process. Who will participate? Will it be a group of people, and if so who will

FIGURE 7.1. A PROCESS FOR SELECTING COURSES TO DELIVER IN AN E-LEARNING MODE.

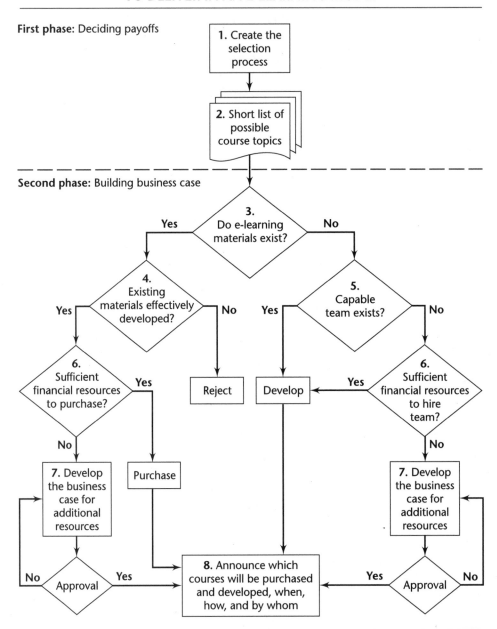

Source: Canadian military. The model is under constant review and revision by the military. Each organization must select the model and criteria it uses for choosing training to deliver in an e-learning mode.

be in the group? What skills will participants require? Will the group make recommendations to a higher authority that will make the final decision?

Whatever your process, make certain that the main stakeholders are consulted. Your decision must be supported by your organization and must be credible to stakeholders. Also, the selection process has to fit the culture of your organization. The normal processes, understood and respected, that are followed for approval of budgets and other items should be paralleled in the e-learning selection process. Use clear selection criteria. The information in this chapter can help you set these for your particular group.

Once you have set clear selection criteria, form a representative team and give it a mandate to make recommendations. Committee members must have strong knowledge of existing training, along with extensive knowledge of e-learning. External consultants can round out representation from the internal team and offer a broad perspective and up-to-date market information. Ultimately, the group's deliberations will be conveyed to senior management for consideration and approval.

2. Short List of Possible Course Topics

Once the selection process is set, you need a starting point. Does your organization wish to consider all of its existing courses for e-learning or are there priority areas? A place to start is to review what has happened to date with technology–assisted learning. Which undertakings have been most successful? Where have there been problems? What units in your organization are supportive? Where is there the most to gain from e-learning? What existing training is not going well and could be converted to e-learning? What existing training is going very well? Should it be removed from consideration at the present time for conversion to e-learning? Start the process by considering a limited number of topics. A review of everything that is available could absorb an inordinate amount of resources. So be selective.

Topics Rating Factors. Exhibit 7.1 below provides an example of how to rate your courses. It lists factors to consider in your initial analysis. You might start by examining twelve topics, for example, and gradually narrow the number to four or five. The same approach could just as well be applied to larger units, such as "programs," or to smaller ones, such as the short elements of instruction sometimes called "learning objects" or "knowledge nuggets."

EXHIBIT 7.1. SAMPLE COURSE TOPICS RATING SHEET COMPLETED FOR FIVE TOPICS.

Factors	Courses				
	1	**2**	**3**	**4**	**5**
Management					
Increases the number of people trained to perform a job	5	4	5	3	2
Improves quality of life for participants and families	5	4	3	5	4
Increases capacity to produce outputs	4	4	3	2	3
Addresses skill shortages in critical occupations	4	3	2	2	2
Is a priority item for the organization	5	4	3	2	2
Can be developed using the rapid prototyping approach	5	4	3	3	3
Reduces travel and accommodation costs	4	2	3	4	3
Reduces training overhead	4	5	4	3	4
Subtotal	36	30	26	24	23
Learning					
Enhances ease of access	3	4	3	4	4
Provides an effective approach for learners	4	3	3	4	4
Can be delivered anywhere, including in an operational context	5	3	3	5	5
Provides for refresher training on demand	4	4	4	3	4
Can be delivered just-in-time	4	5	4	3	2
Subtotal	20	19	17	19	19
Existing Training Materials					
Are current	5	4	3	3	3
Are suitable for adapting to e-learning	5	4	3	3	3
Subtotal	10	8	6	6	6
Learners					
Potential students are ready for e-learning	5	4	3	3	3
Tasks to be taught are critical for operational effectiveness	5	3	3	3	3
Subtotal	10	7	6	6	6
For Self-Paced					
Content is stable and does not require frequent updating	5	2	3	3	3
For Instructor-Led					
Content is dynamic and requires frequent updating	2	5	3	3	3

Assessing Potential Payoff. In Exhibit 7.1, fictitious ratings are given to five topics that are being considered for conversion to e-learning. The topics are rated on a scale of 1 to 5, with the following criteria: 1 is very low; 2 is low; 3 is medium; 4 is high; and 5 is very high. Note that no weightings have been assigned to any of the items. Critical items may also have to be weighted. For example, in some situations, throughput is a major consideration; therefore it would not be fair to rate it at the same level as some other items on the checklist. You could give more weight by scoring out of ten.

Topic 1 is deemed the most suitable for e-learning on the sample worksheet. It was scored high on the self-paced scale, so it could be delivered in that mode. Topic 2 was scored next overall. It was scored high in a leader-led mode and it could be developed as a leader-led course. Even with the data on the sample, however, we are not ready to make a final decision. We must first determine whether there are existing materials that could be used in the course in lieu of developing materials from the ground up.

3. Do e-Learning Materials Exist?

The use of existing materials can save an organization time, money, and resources. Also, vendors may have the very course materials you require, especially if you are addressing soft skills or generic topics such as harassment, safety, conflict resolution, business management procedures, and similar areas. Or another organization might have developed materials you can use. You could perhaps arrange a swap through a professional organization where you meet people with interests similar to yours.

4. Are Existing Materials Effectively Developed?

After you have identified existing materials, the next question is how to know whether they are sound. This question applies to situations in which you are considering leasing, purchasing, or converting existing conventional or e-learning materials to your particular situation. You could consult a vendor or service that rates materials, such as Lguide.com. If you do, how do you know that you can trust the advice you receive? You want to be certain that the existing materials are sound. Normally we recommend that the quality of the materials be evaluated by test-driving them, checking the design process followed, and interviewing people who have used them. Exhibit 7.2 is a tool you can use to assess existing materials that you are considering purchasing. Again, this is not a prescribed approach. Adapt the checklist to your situation.

EXHIBIT 7.2. CHECKLIST FOR EVALUATING MATERIALS.

Course Name: _____

Provider: _____ *Cost:* _____

Evaluated by: _____

System used for evaluating: _____ *Date:* _____

Minimum recommended system: _____

Overall Approach of Materials	**Yes**	**No**
Blends e-learning with conventional learning	☐	☐
Delivered via the Web	☐	☐
Delivered via CD-ROM	☐	☐
Leader-led synchronous	☐	☐
Leader-led asynchronous	☐	☐
Self-paced	☐	☐
Self-paced with coaches or mentors	☐	☐
Informal learning (information without a specific instructional strategy)	☐	☐
Can be linked to competencies	☐	☐
Includes a pre-assessment	☐	☐

Score the remaining criteria

Content

Selection Criteria	**High**	**Medium**	**Low**
The information in the course is	☐	☐	☐
Accurate, up-to-date	☐	☐	☐
Clearly explained (well-organized and well-written)	☐	☐	☐
Presented in the learners' context	☐	☐	☐
Deals with need to know, not nice to know	☐	☐	☐

	High	Medium	Low

Instructional Design

	High	Medium	Low
Gains attention	☐	☐	☐
Informs learners of objectives	☐	☐	☐
Achievable objectives	☐	☐	☐
Measured objectives	☐	☐	☐
Objectives reflect what learners need to know	☐	☐	☐
Stimulates recall of prior learning	☐	☐	☐
Presents the content	☐	☐	☐
Supports varied learning styles	☐	☐	☐
Materials are visually appealing	☐	☐	☐
Provides learning guidance	☐	☐	☐
Elicits performance (practice)	☐	☐	☐
Provides realistic opportunities to practice skills	☐	☐	☐
Provides feedback	☐	☐	☐
Assess performance	☐	☐	☐
Enhances retention and transfer to the job	☐	☐	☐
Provides helpful additional resources and tools or links to them	☐	☐	☐
Provides help	☐	☐	☐

1. How is attention gained? _____

Technology

	High	Medium	Low
Easy-to-use interface	☐	☐	☐
Plug-in or other software not required	☐	☐	☐
Learners can control the flow by skipping or repeating sections	☐	☐	☐
Instructors voice and or image are clear, and helpful	☐	☐	☐

Overall Value

	High	Medium	Low
The content is worth the time and money required to learn it	☐	☐	☐
Includes online help	☐	☐	☐
You would recommend the course to a colleague	☐	☐	☐

2. What are the pricing arrangements? _____

Totals	**x 3**	**x 2**	**x 1**
	____	____	____

If the materials you locate are available in a shareable courseware format, you will be able to embed them in new materials you are developing. If the materials are embedded as links, they will be updated automatically when the original materials are modified.

5. Does a Capable Team Exist?

If there are no existing materials or if the existing ones are not suitable, you must develop your own. An e-learning development team consists of several essential members: managers, project managers, instructors, developers, technical experts, and subject-matter experts (SMEs). The absence of capable people to fill all of these slots will diminish the success of e-learning. If the team members are not available internally, contract with external consultants to fill the gaps. You can learn about the availability of consultants through professional associations, trade publications, and Internet resources.

6. Are There Sufficient Financial Resources?

In the short run, annual budgets might be a determining factor in the selection of training to deliver in an e-learning mode. However, it is also important to take a long-range view. The best e-learning initiative, the one that produces the best results and has the most profound impact on your organization, could also be beyond your present budget. Opportunity funds could become available at the end of the fiscal year, or additional funds could be acquired to support this long-range view. Although we describe a micromanagement process below, it is important to keep the high-level view in mind.

7. Develop the Business Case for Additional Resources

The flowchart in Figure 7.1 illustrates that a business case must be developed if there are not sufficient funds to purchase or develop e-learning courses or materials. Where internal guidelines for developing a business case for training already exist, they should be used for e-learning initiatives.

8. Announce Decisions

The information gathered and decisions made above are then converted to a work plan and communicated to stakeholders, who will want to know which course will be developed, when, how, and by whom.

Assessment Checklists

It is sometimes said that the difficulty of making a decision increases proportionately as the number of options increases. The Web is wonderful in the sense that it delivers more options to your desktop, but more options can create a decision-making nightmare. Here are four checklists to adapt to your particular situation when selecting e-learning courseware.

e-Learning Options Checklist

The checklist below provides a list of options to use when selecting e-learning courseware. It was developed with self-paced e-learning in mind, but you can use it for other types of e-learning with minimal modification. The intent is to provide sample areas that can be selected for evaluating software. An assessment tool would normally include some, not all of the twenty-eight items listed on this particular checklist. The checklist is divided into sections on "learners," "courseware design," "management," and "other factors."

EXHIBIT 7.3. E-LEARNING OPTIONS CHECKLIST

Criteria	Description	High	Medium	Low
Learners				
1. Feedback	Learners receive timely and pertinent feedback on how well they are progressing	☐	☐	☐
2. Help	Learners can access a help screen about instructional material and technical issues at any time	☐	☐	☐

Criteria	Description	High	Medium	Low
3. Learner control	Courseware has a recommended path and the freedom for learners to select an alternative path	☐	☐	☐
4. Motivation	Courseware engages students to participate in a timely fashion	☐	☐	☐
5. Relevant	Importance and relevance of material being taught is highlighted	☐	☐	☐
6. Support materials	Learner guide, job aids, reference material, and so forth, available as required	☐	☐	☐
7. User friendly	Interface and navigation are similar to what users are familiar with and are easy to access	☐	☐	☐

Courseware Design

Criteria	Description	High	Medium	Low
8. Chunking	Content organized into convenient modules that are in line with what learners need to know and can absorb in the time they have available for e-learning	☐	☐	☐
9. Directions	Instructions are concise, flow logically, and contain examples	☐	☐	☐
10. Interface	Design is consistent throughout	☐	☐	☐
11. Learner involvement	Learner uses knowledge and skill in job-related tasks	☐	☐	☐
12. Media	Enhance learning	☐	☐	☐
13. Objectives	Made clear to learners at the start of each major learning activity; course content addresses the objectives	☐	☐	☐
14. Writing	Content is clearly written and accurate	☐	☐	☐

Management

Criteria	Description	High	Medium	Low
15. Availability	Instructional materials are available to the students 24/7	☐	☐	☐
16. Installation	Courseware is easy to install and remove from network/system	☐	☐	☐
17. Plug-ins	Uses common plug-ins that are supported and are easy to obtain and install	☐	☐	☐

Criteria	Description	High	Medium	Low
18. Security	Unauthorized people cannot gain access to courseware and management data	☐	☐	☐
19. Student data	Courseware tracks learners' participation and progress	☐	☐	☐
20. Technical requirements	Connect speed permits smooth flow of data	☐	☐	☐
21. Technical support staff	Technical training available; technical help desk available 24/7	☐	☐	☐
Other Factors				
22. Configuration	Courseware configured as shareable courseware objects to allow for rapid reuse	☐	☐	☐
23. Reviews	Reviewers made positive comments about the learning materials	☐	☐	☐
24. Value	High value compared to other products	☐	☐	☐
25. Blended approach	Courseware is part of a blended approach using conventional and e-learning and several types of e-learning	☐	☐	☐
26. Menus	Fewer than three levels of menus so that users can readily move around, retrace their steps, and not become lost or confused	☐	☐	☐
27. Bookmarking	A bookmarking feature allows students to know what they have finished and return to where they left off	☐	☐	☐
28. Menus	Easy to use, that is, seven items or fewer to facilitate rapid selection	☐	☐	☐

Tool 2: Evaluation Sheet for Vendor Courseware

The tool reproduced in Exhibit 7.4 was developed in the Canadian military to assess existing courseware from vendors. The items in this evaluation instrument reflect what one organization considered important. You may revise the form by adding additional criteria from earlier sections of this chapter.

EXHIBIT 7.4. SAMPLE E-LEARNING REVIEW SHEET.

Course Name: _____ ABC—Level 1 _____

Provider: _____ ACMEWARE _____ *Cost:* _____

Evaluator: _____ J. Tester _____

System Used: _____ ARMADA E500 _____ *Date:* _____

Overall Approach of Materials	**Yes**	**No**	**Uncertain***
Blends e-learning with conventional learning	☐	☐	☐
Delivered via the Web	☒	☐	☐
Delivered via CD-ROM	☐	☐	☐
Leader-led synchronous	☐	☐	☐
Leader-led asynchronous	☒	☐	☐
Self-paced	☐	☐	☐
Self-paced with coaches or mentors	☐	☐	☐
Informal learning (information without a specific instructional strategy)	☐	☐	☐
Uses sound	☐	☐	☐
Uses animation	☐	☐	☐
Can be linked to competencies	☐	☐	☐
Can be modified to reflect an organization's content	☐	☐	☐
Includes a pre-assessment	☐	☐	☐

Score the remaining criteria as high, medium, or low.

Content

Selection Criteria	**High**	**Medium**	**Low**	**Uncertain**
The information in the course is				
Accurate, up-to-date	☒	☐	☐	☐
Clearly explained (well-organized and well-written)	☒	☐	☐	☐
Presented in the learners' context	☒	☐	☐	☐
Deals with need to know, not nice to know	☒	☐	☐	☐
Instructional Design				
Achievable objectives	☐	☐	☐	☒
Measured objectives	☐	☐	☐	☒

	High	**Medium**	**Low**	**Uncertain**
Provides realistic opportunities to practice skills	☒	☐	☐	☐
Supports varied learning styles	☒	☐	☐	☐
Provides helpful additional resources and tools or links to them	☒	☐	☐	☐
Materials are visually appealing	☒	☐	☐	☐
Engages the learners' attention	☒	☐	☐	☐
How is the learners' attention gained?				

Technology

	High	**Medium**	**Low**	**Uncertain**
Easy-to-use interface	☒	☐	☐	☐
Plug-in or other software not required	☒	☐	☐	☐
Learners can control the flow by skipping or repeating sections	☒	☐	☐	☐
Instructor's voice and/or image are clear and helpful	☒	☐	☐	☐

Overall Value

	High	**Medium**	**Low**	**Uncertain**
The content is worth the time and money required to learn it	☒	☐	☐	☐
Would recommend the course to a colleague	☒	☐	☐	☐
Totals	**15 x 3**	**0 x 2**	**0 x 1**	
	45	**0**	**0**	

Additional Comments

ABC-Level 1 scored 45. Other similar products from the vendors scored at least five points lower. I recommend purchasing ABC-Level 1.

Scored 45. Strong recommendation to purchase.

Application and Adaptation

The models used in this chapter provide insight into how organizations have approached the difficult question of selecting training courses to deliver in an e-learning mode. They raise the fundamental questions that you will need to think through as your organization decides whether to lease, purchase, convert, or build e-learning from scratch. The processes laid out here show but the first steps. You will have to adapt them to your organization's needs. The checklists need to be examined, discussed, tested, and tweaked. Coming up with the final selection tool will take time and effort, but the reward will be worth the hard work.

Test Drive

Select a demo course from one of the leading vendors. Review selection criteria listed on the evaluation grid in Exhibit 7.5. Revise the grid to fit the priorities of the organization you are working with. Use the revised grid to evaluate the course.

EXHIBIT 7.5. E-LEARNING REVIEW SHEET.

Course Name: _____

Provider: _____ *Cost:* _____

Evaluator: _____

System Used: _____ *Date:* _____

Overall Approach of Materials	**Yes**	**No**	**Uncertain**
Blends e-learning with conventional learning	☐	☐	☐
Delivered via the Web	☐	☐	☐
Delivered via CD-ROM	☐	☐	☐
Leader-led synchronous	☐	☐	☐
Leader-led asynchronous	☐	☐	☐
Self-paced	☐	☐	☐
Self-paced with coaches or mentors	☐	☐	☐
Informal learning (information without a specific instructional strategy)	☐	☐	☐
Uses sound	☐	☐	☐
Uses animation	☐	☐	☐
Can be linked to competencies	☐	☐	☐
Can be modified to reflect an organization's content	☐	☐	☐
Includes a pre-assessment	☐	☐	☐

Score the remaining criteria as high, medium, or low.

Content

Selection Criteria	**High**	**Medium**	**Low**	**Uncertain**
The information in the course is				
Accurate, up-to-date	☐	☐	☐	☐
Clearly explained (well-organized and well-written)	☐	☐	☐	☐
Presented in the learners' context	☐	☐	☐	☐
Deals with need to know, not nice to know	☐	☐	☐	☐

Instructional Design

	High	**Medium**	**Low**	**Uncertain**
Achievable objectives	☐	☐	☐	☐
Measured objectives	☐	☐	☐	☐

	High	Medium	Low	Uncertain
Provides realistic opportunities to practice skills	☐	☐	☐	☐
Supports varied learning styles	☐	☐	☐	☐
Provides helpful additional resources and tools or links to them	☐	☐	☐	☐
Materials are visually appealing	☐	☐	☐	☐
Engages the learners' attention	☐	☐	☐	☐

How is the learners' attention gained?

Technology

	High	Medium	Low	Uncertain
Easy-to-use interface	☐	☐	☐	☐
Plug-in or other software not required	☐	☐	☐	☐
Learners can control the flow by skipping or repeating sections	☐	☐	☐	☐
Instructor's voice and/or image are clear and helpful	☐	☐	☐	☐

Overall Value

	High	Medium	Low	Uncertain
The content is worth the time and money required to learn it	☐	☐	☐	☐
Would recommend the course to a colleague	☐	☐	☐	☐
Totals	**x 3**	**x 2**	**x 1**	
	____	____	____	

Additional Comments

CHAPTER EIGHT

VIRTUAL CLASSROOMS

Delivering Courses Online

In the conventional training world, the phrase *deliver training* means to conduct training. An instructor, for example, delivers training by presenting a lesson in a classroom. In the e-learning world, the word *deliver* has a broader meaning. e-Learning, both self-paced and leader-led, is often accessed by a learner through a software system called a learning management system (LMS), a content management systems (CMS), or some other type of database or management system.

There are a number of tasks associated with your LMS software that every organization will have to learn, for example: how to upload training to the system as well as how to register students, track participation, generate reports, and other features, depending on what the system offers. Software vendors provide this training. It is important that people who will be managing the training and using the delivery system take the training and understand the full range of services offered by the LMS software.

The delivery role associated with pure self-paced training is the administrative one mentioned above. However, self-paced training is often blended with leader-led e-learning, whereby a coach, for example, might work with the learners as they progress through the self-paced modules. In any leader-led scenario, the delivery role is broad and complex.

This chapter explores the leader-led delivery role. It will help to prepare you to work as an online instructor, facilitator, or coach or, if you are a training developer or manager, to understand what the role entails. It will also be of assistance if you already have experience with online instruction, are a bit frustrated, and would like to find ways to tweak your skills. We use the term *instructor* throughout this chapter for consistency, but in many cases the role of an online instructor is not to instruct in the traditional stand-up mode but to lead, to mediate, to coach, and to facilitate learning.

From Access to Development, Step by Step

We introduced Gilly Salmon's five-phase model for online learning in Chapter Six during our discussion of learning theory and e-learning. Here we look at each phase from the perspectives of both learner and instructor, focusing on how the learner progresses to increased independence through the instructor's actions (Figure 8.1).

Stage One: Access and Motivation

Students have to be able to access the system. The role of the instructor at this stage is to welcome students, to motivate them, and to direct them to sources of help for gaining access to the system. Responses by the instructor at this stage are largely to the individual and may be through email rather than through threaded discussion.

Learner progress: At this point, learners often have trouble using a threaded discussion properly and it may take a fair bit of patience to teach them how to do it correctly.

Typical posting: Post everything that is meant for the threaded discussion to email to ensure that all learners see it, especially novice e-learners.

Stage Two: Online Socialization

Learners start to appreciate the social environment of the online discussion. They are also learning how to participate effectively. At this stage the instructor helps them make the successful transition to e-learning. As each learner is still finding his or her way around, responses by the instructor are still largely individual but may be on the threaded discussion and therefore public. However, learners may still need individual support via e-mail.

FIGURE 8.1. SALMON'S FIVE-PHASE MODEL FOR ONLINE LEARNING.

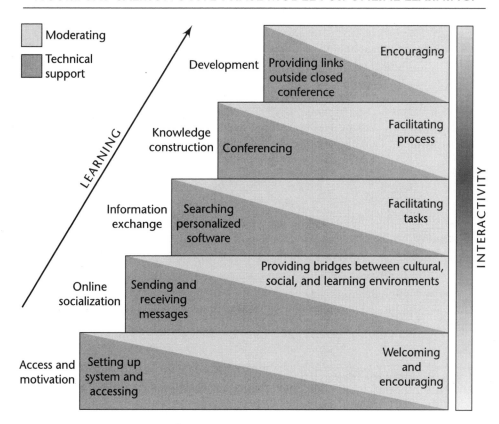

Learner progress: At this time some learners will start to interact with others but not all will be comfortable doing this.

Typical posting: Raise a question about a posting and invite others to participate, for example: "Has anyone thought of what might be the underlying cause of the observation by X?"

Stage Three: Information Exchange

The learners start to appreciate the benefits of e-learning. There are rich online resources, and online discussions can be stimulating. The instructor acts as research leader and supporter in assisting learners to find the information they are seeking. Instructor responses are often to the whole group.

Instructors might be pointing out Web sites at this point that are related to topics the learners have raised. Instructors will continue to add value to discussions, focusing on postings that engage the entire group.

Learner progress: Learners are highly engaged both in discussing and in seeking other learning resources online.

Typical posting: Post an individual message to a learner recommending a Web site, for example: "You will find additional information about this topic at X. Does anyone else have Web sites to recommend on this topic?"

Stage Four: Knowledge Construction

Instructors and learners are working together to generate and make new meanings through their collaboration. The instructor stimulates and facilitates this interaction. Instructors post questions that encourage analysis. They help to lead learners to new levels of observation.

Learner progress: Learners are full partners in high-level learning (that is, analysis, synthesis, and evaluation).

Typical posting: "We have now heard from four people on this topic. Do any of you see trends you would like to point out?"

Stage Five: Development

Learners are becoming independent online and the instructor encourages this independence. The instructor withdraws as the learners become more self-directed. Instructors continue to observe postings and might post individual email messages to encourage participation.

Learner progress: Independence.

Typical posting: Nothing.

A New Role for Instructors

e-Learning instructors, like e-learning itself, come in different flavors. In some variations of self-paced e-learning, instructors play a coaching role, assisting students learning in a self-study mode. Some organizations, such as Canada's Department of Foreign Affairs, introduced self-paced courses without coaches and then added them, ensuring that e-learning had a human touch. Software vendor SmartForce also noted the gap created by not having human contact in e-learning and subsequently added online coaches to self-paced materials.

Instructors play a central role in leader-led e-learning, either delivering presentations or moderating discussions. In a synchronous delivery situation, the instructor delivers content to learners in real time using a Web camera, the telephone, or some other direct communication medium. In an asynchronous mode, instructors set up the topics for discussion, introduce them, and moderate the goings on. The communications between learners and instructors occur via some delayed means, normally a *threaded discussion*—a place on the Internet where instructors and students pose questions and seek answers. These discussions go by a variety of names, including forums, online communities, and discussion areas. Their overall objective is to help participants to explore new ideas.

Basic Skills

Successful classroom leaders have the basic skills required to teach online. They know how to introduce topics, engage participants, move topics along, and summarize discussions. Combine these basic skills with a solid knowledge of computers and the learning management system through which they will deliver online learning, and it may look like they are all set. The only problem is that one's ability to lead face-to-face discussions is probably based on being able to see participants, read their nonverbal signals, and influence their participation by using one's own nonverbal signals.

Unfortunately, there are normally no nonverbal signals, or very few, in both asynchronous and synchronous e-learning. Therefore, it is hard, especially in asynchronous e-learning, to judge how people feel. In addition, it may be hard for an online instructor to lead a group without feedback from learners that shows their feelings about and understanding of the material. The closest things in an e-learning environment are *emoticons*, the different variations on a happy face that are used to convey emotions. (See box.)

Emoticons: e-Learning Nonverbals

Some common emoticons used to express emotion in asynchronous e-learning follow:

:-)	basic smile	=)	glazed over	;-D	big smile
:-(	frown	;-)	wink		

Synchronous e-learning also has its challenges. Normally, instructors delivering a live webcast cannot see participants unless they are using a sophisticated system that places cameras in the room where participants are grouped. Also, synchronous e-learning presents a host of technical challenges associated with putting all the technology in place, ensuring that everyone has the required technology, and conducting the session.

> "Technically, the course was not prepared properly, so we were playing around with technical things when we should have been receiving instruction. Instructors were very, very positive and they worked very, very hard to keep things going, but they did not have a methodology to present the course. So we all suffered."   —Tom, an online student

While online learning can be a new and challenging experience for instructors, the same is true for learners. They are exposed to the discussion, but chances are they do not really know much about the people who are making the comments. It is like hobnobbing blindfolded at a cocktail party. There are many opportunities for interaction and communication, but when you cannot see people's faces it is hard to know where to start. Learners, like instructors, miss the nonverbal clues that encourage them to engage with the instructor and with one another. It's not easy to be an e-learner.

Fortunately, people have had enough experience with moderating e-learning that a body of literature is blossoming. Writers with several years' experience in the field have crafted some excellent books about synchronous and asynchronous e-learning in both academic and workplace contexts. Even better, many leading authors have placed excellent articles online. (See the list of resources at the end of this chapter.)

Guide on the Side Facilitation

Many online instructors limit themselves to using only two or three approaches, rather than using the full range of approaches that are available. There is good evidence that productive online discussion results from moderators cautiously intervening in the process and not simply serving as subject-matter experts. In more colorful words, successful online facilitation is more likely from using the "guide on the side" style, rather than from being a "sage on the stage" (Collision, Elbaum, Haavind, & Tinker, 2000). Table 8.1 outlines six "guide on the side" approaches available to online facilitators in either a synchronous or an asynchronous mode.

TABLE 8.1. SIX "GUIDE ON THE SIDE" FACILITATION APPROACHES.

Role	Action	Results
Starter	Lays out the spectrum of possible responses	Broadens the scope of the discussion
Conceptual facilitator	Draws abstractions from the discussion	Can raise the level of a discussion; appeals to participants who enjoy playing with ideas
Reflective guide	Comments on the implications of comments made by participants	Can bridge to a practical application of the material being discussed, which can engage students and lead to application of what is being learned
Personal muse	Questions own views	Tends to legitimize critiquing the instructor's views and in that way opens up the discussion
Mediator	When participants are disagreeing, focuses the discussion on common ground	Tends to help build consensus and move the discussion away from debate to finding common solutions
Role player	Assumes role of another person	By playfully assuming a role, such as a teacher on Monday flush with new ideas, presents alternative perspectives without concern for personal ownership or direct confrontation with participants

Source: G. Collision, B. Elbaum, S. Haavind, & R. Tinker, *Facilitating Online Learning: Effective Strategies for Moderators.* Madison, WI: Atwood Publishing, 2000.

By being aware of the six roles described in Table 8.1 and adopting different ones from time to time in postings to a threaded discussion, instructors can vary their tone and keep the discussion moving.

One of the underlying ideas is to avoid playing the expert all of the time. Online instructors who assume that role by taking a strong stand tend to inhibit discussion among the less vocal participants. There are other instructor actions that tend to undermine productive discussion, for example, asking too many questions or dominating the discussion to the exclusion of many of the learners. Table 8.2 lists some of these actions and their possible results.

TABLE 8.2. WAYS INSTRUCTORS UNDERMINE ONLINE DISCUSSION.

Instructor Actions	**Possible Results**
Instructors join a debate and assume a position	Instructors undermine the possibility of learners' taking ownership for a discussion
Instructors enjoy being in the middle of an online discussion	Instructors may dominate the dialogue and undermine the full participation of learners
Instructor asks too many questions	Students have a tendency to treat all questions as important and become swamped with clever questions posed by the instructor
Instructors play up their own expertise or experience	Participants have a tendency to tune out to a "sage on the stage"

Competency Development for Online Instructors

Obviously, online instructors need a number of competencies. If your organization does not have much experience with e-learning and you must develop online instructors, it is important to assess the potential of other members of the organization to become effective online instructors. The new competencies you seek will include:

- A willingness to step back from the limelight and facilitate learning
- An openness to learn new approaches to learning
- Ability to monitor personal progress and take action to improve skills
- Appreciation of the benefits of e-learning
- Creativity to design and adapt e-learning for various purposes, groups, and topics

- The ability to write clear email messages
- The ability to anticipate learner reactions to situations
- The ability to learn online facilitation skills
- Time management skills
- The ability to support and counsel others through email

If you assess members of your organization and you do not find people with the exact skills listed above, one option is to identify in-house people who possess three higher level competencies that indicate they can further develop the other skills. The higher level skills and attitudes are

- Empathy
- Flexibility
- Eagerness to become an online instructor

If you still come up short, two additional options are (1) to recruit new instructors from outside your organization or (2) to outsource the function by engaging consultants or contract workers to deliver the e-learning program. The following cases illustrate how others have resolved these issues.

Case 1: A Classroom Instructor Goes Online

When a leading college approached Vicky[1] to teach her regular classroom course online, she enthusiastically accepted. e-Learning presented an opportunity to work from her home office and at the same time to deal with students worldwide, teaching a subject she loves and understands in great depth. Along the way, Vicky faced several issues. Here are some of the main ones and the solutions she developed working with a team of professionals.

Keeping Costs Down

Vicky's course does not have the large potential clientele that a general arts course would have, or for that matter a course about computer software. Because enrollment revenue forecasts were small, Vicky had to manage costs tightly. There were no funds for rich multimedia or for extensive instructional design. Consequently, the course was primarily text-based. Over time, however, she has added videos.

Fostering Interactivity

When a course is primarily text-based, one must be concerned that it is essentially an electronic page turner with little educational value added. Vicky knows that the most effective online courses emulate a classroom situation, so she was committed to making her course interactive with the help of the college design and development team.

For example, text-based lectures have been supplemented by six videos. Two were produced for the course and four are from equipment manufacturers. Before starting the course, participants receive a video of the instructor enthusiastically explaining the course. For a critical section about focus groups, Vicky also led the production of a video. In both cases, students pop the videos into a VCR and view them on a monitor. Although the monitor is good for viewing the information because it has a large screen, the participants' TV and VCR are often not in the same room as their computers. To overcome this inconvenience, the college has placed the videos onto a CD to make it easier for students to access the information on the videos at the same time as they use the other material on their computer.

Evaluating Students

Online learning might sound free and easy. Surf the Net. Join chat groups when you feel like it. Study at the beach. Some students register for online learning thinking it is easier than the classroom version. They don't last long. Online learning is at least as demanding as classroom learning, and perhaps even more demanding on students' time, creativity, and energy. More than 20 percent of people dropped out of Vicky's first course in the first week.

Vicky incorporated several formal evaluations into her course, consisting of six assignments (three individual, three team). The first assignment was to develop a team protocol. The group had to decide how they would function.

Finding Meaningful Assignments

In classroom versions of courses like Vicky conducts, instructors like to end with a group exercise in which participants make presentations to management. This type of activity summarizes the course well, provides instructors a chance to assess students' learning, and helps students to integrate essential

Ten Tips for Managing Instructors' Time

Online courses are not like classroom courses where there is a fixed framework governed by classroom and seminar times and the instructor's and learners' availability for meetings. In online learning, email messages can be sent to instructors at any time of the day. But eager instructors who respond to every learner individually find themselves spending three times as many hours instructing an online course as a regular classroom course.

Some of the solutions Vicky and others have found to deal with these challenges follow:

1. *Keep the number of learners to a manageable size.* For some courses this will mean ten students. For others it might be up to twenty, depending on how much interactivity the course requires and the eagerness of students to participate.
2. *Encourage the use of discussion forums with the threaded discussion feature.* That way, participants can consult the messages that have been posted and see how a discussion developed.
3. *Make good use of technical resources.* If you use synchronous chat discussions, for example, work with your technical people to find a way to save the chat discussions and place them where people can review what has been said.
4. *Structure the times when interactivity occurs.* For example, set up chat arrangements whereby all students are expected to participate at a specific time.
5. *Keep the needs of the group in mind when communicating with individual learners.* If a student asks a question that could come from other students later, ask the student if it is okay to share the answer with the entire class.
6. *Foster learner interaction.* Encourage students to communicate among themselves through synchronous and asynchronous tools.
7. *Discourage going offline.* In order to keep everyone focused on the course plan, discourage students from communicating offline through email.
8. *Keep things on track.* Monitor the public discussions on bulletin boards and provide assistance when people get off the topic or fail to understand essential course content.
9. *Present a structured course.* To some extent, a Web site and the hyperlinks of html encourage, or even force, structure. However, instructors must keep working on structure. One useful approach is to provide assignments and discussion questions ahead of when they are needed so that students can prepare in advance. Some keen students will type up their thoughts in advance and do a cut and paste in the synchronous and asynchronous sessions. This can save time and help them make their points more effectively.
10. *Have a contingency plan.* Make it clear that people can use the phone, fax, or other modes of communication when their computers are down. Ensure that the mechanisms are in place to allow that to happen.

Practical Advice to Learners

Vicky and other colleagues developed practical advice for learners. Here are some of their ideas and tips to learners from their Web site.

Welcome to a New Experience

Learning by distance is a new experience for many people. Working as a team and communicating by email and through the Internet is even newer! The members of some teams may not be located in the same city or even the same time zone! While you are expected to know how to get online and to be familiar with communicating via the Internet, here are some suggestions that may help you and your team members manage your learning, your team work, and communication with other participants more effectively.

Suggestions for Managing Team Work

A discussion area will be set up for your team so that team members can sign on and make any comments, observations, or suggestions about the assignment. Establish an online meeting schedule so that team members can rely on meeting on a regular basis.

- For each assignment, it is suggested that you meet online before you begin the assignment to confirm the team's understanding of the task and to outline an approach to the assignment.
- Appoint a team leader for each assignment. The team leader will coordinate communication, set a schedule for and facilitate online team meetings, assure that tasks are assigned to each team member and that a schedule for completion of all tasks is determined, and follow up with any team member who misses a meeting or deadline. (*Note:* team leader designation rotates to another team member for each assignment.)
- Appoint an editor for each assignment. The task of the editor is to combine the work of each of the team members into a whole. For example, the team may decide to delegate different parts of the assignment to different team members rather than have the whole team work on the whole assignment.
- The editor will synthesize the work of each of the team members into one "product," ensure there is continuity and flow throughout the assignment, and check for grammatical and spelling errors. (*Note:* editor designation rotates to another team member for each assignment.)
- If the team decides to approach the assignment as a whole rather than splitting the assignment into individual tasks, the team leader will facilitate the meeting, but the editor will organize group input and produce a first draft for the others to consider.

- Once a final draft has been completed, the editor will upload it to the team's discussion area and the team leader will convene an online team meeting to discuss the draft and make changes.
- The editor will then revise the assignment or have team members revise their respective task areas and submit these changes for the editor to produce a final assignment.
- The team leader will convene another online team meeting to discuss the final document, after which the editor makes final changes and submits the document to the instructor and other teams for evaluation.

Remember, these are suggestions only and you may wish to establish different team protocol for managing the assignments in this course.

learning from the course. But using the Web to accomplish this requires a fresh approach.

Solutions can be found by thinking through the complete situation, knowing your goals, mastering the technology, or obtaining good advice. Know the technology available to your students. Try out different approaches. And build from there.

There are now several ways to deliver voice and images over the Web and, in that way, replicate some of the classroom's interactivity. An inexpensive Web camera attached to a computer allows an instructor to develop videos that can be recorded and distributed through a Web site using streaming video software. Or a presentation can be viewed live using a Web camera and software. A less high-tech solution is to set up a PowerPoint® presentation on the Web and use a telephone bridge line. Yet another approach is to use the services of a vendor who provides a service to integrate voice (either over the telephone or over the Internet) with presentations in software such as PowerPoint.

Vicky chose to use the telephone bridge line combined with PowerPoint solution because several students in her course had the limited bandwidth that 56K dial-up lines offer. The challenge for instructors in this example and on a regular basis is to come up with scenarios that emulate the real thing and that are within the technology available to all students.

> "I am a young woman. I studied online. Other course participants were older men. On the Web I felt fully accepted. In a classroom, I think they would have made me feel less accepted and my ideas would have received less consideration."   —Online learning participant

Dealing with People from Diverse Backgrounds

Online instructors find that people from diverse backgrounds enroll in their programs. These can be people from many locations around the world, different age groups, various levels of education, and different levels of knowledge of the subject matters.

Vicky finds that once participants know who else is in the group and their own relative place within the group, they help each other. For example, the more experienced students provide stories from their backgrounds. Younger, perhaps more academically inclined students, ask pertinent questions. In the end, student diversity is a positive element of Vicky's courses.

Gaining Credibility

Online instructors must have broad, practical knowledge of the subject they are teaching as well as strong theoretical knowledge. They need both because their students will be looking for both. In the end, however, concrete experiences help make learning stick. Vicky finds that her stories about real-world experiences help her build exercises that simulate real-world situations and aid practical application of what is learned.

Using Facilitation Skills

Online instructors need to learn to watch an online discussion brew and jump in at the appropriate time. Online facilitation may require one to be firm at times, laissez-faire at others. In the end, the online instructor needs to create a supportive environment where all students feel comfortable participating. Moreover, the students need to feel supported by an understanding, knowledgeable, accessible instructor.

Vicky finds that she has developed a new sensitivity to the way people write online. She misses seeing their faces and body movements as they speak;

however, she finds that her new ability to read between the lines helps her to keep a nurturing eye on her students.

Case 2: A Failed Webcast

In Utopia there would be no failed webcasts. Every chapter of this book would gush e-learning success stories. Sorry, it's not that way. Problems happen. This story is not meant to embarrass the people who tried to demonstrate the effectiveness of a webcast. We present it so that others can learn from what went wrong.

The plan was to conduct a ninety-minute webcast on a Wednesday at 12 noon. The purpose of the online seminar was to examine issues associated with converting traditional classroom teaching to online courses. The presenter, let's call her Helga, was setting out to advise viewers of both pros and cons from the end user's perspective, as well as from the instructor and IT service viewpoints.

It promised to be an intriguing play within a play—using e-learning to explain e-learning. Invitations were sent out to members of two distance learning organizations. The topics sparked considerable interest and some people received half a dozen notices forwarded from others, right up to the time the session was to start. And that was the beginning of the problem. Too many people tried to participate.

Somewhere in the neighborhood of 175 people registered for the webcast by transmission time. Plus, at webcast time, some 325 additional people tried to join the session. The bandwidth could not handle the traffic. People who were logged on were cut off and forced to reload. The snowballing effect was such that precious few saw the complete presentation. Some hapless cybernauts saw only three minutes out of an hour-long webcast.

A discussion forum had been set up for post-session discussion. Needless to say, all of the discussion was about the technology—or lack of adequate technology.

Lessons Learned

A number of administrative actions could have been taken to manage the technology in this case, from simply limiting the number of participants to creating an archival video to run from participants' hard drives later. These and other suggestions from the project team for effectively managing a webcast are summarized in Table 8.3. These insights were gained after the fact by those involved.

TABLE 8.3. LESSONS FROM A FAILED WEBCAST.

Issue	Response
Unexpectedly large numbers of participants clogged the system	Hold your webcast at a time of the day when Web traffic is typically lowest; control the number of registrants by having people sign up in advance; limit the number of people who can sign up; do not allow any registration during the session
Quality of the video was dubious	Consider archiving a video and having people view it asynchronously from their hard drive, not through a synchronous webcast; advise instructors to reduce their body movement when they speak on a video that will be communicated over the Web or online
Online discussion after the session was short-lived and not productive	Register all participants in the online discussion through a listserv; appoint an animator to facilitate the discussion
Once the webcast started there were network problems	Work closely with support people (IS department or software developers) to anticipate network problems and develop contingency plans for real-time resolution
Entire project was done with volunteers	Recognize webcasts as a specialty area and be prepared to invest money and/or plenty of time to learn about it
Unforeseen glitches everywhere	Practice, practice, practice with the tools during development; pilot thoroughly before going live

Conclusions About Online Delivery

At first glance, you might think that teaching online is the same as teaching in the classroom. But online instructors, both synchronous and asynchronous, find they miss the "face time" with participants. They miss the nonverbal messages on participants' faces when they are confused, convinced, or amused and all the other messages we learn to read in people's faces. To compensate for the lack of nonverbal communication, online instructors must develop new facilitation techniques and new sensitivities. We have given you plenty of tips in this chapter. However, acquiring such skills takes practice and time.

Test Drive

You are to meet with a group of classroom instructors who wish to become online instructors, facilitators, and coaches. What advice would you give them based on your experience with e-learning and the information in this chapter?

Online Learning Resources

Berge, Zane L., & Schreiber, Deborah A. (Eds.). *Distance Training: How Innovative Organizations Are Using Technology to Maximize Learning and Meet Business Objectives.* San Francisco: Jossey-Bass, 1999. www.emoderators.com/

Berge, Zane L. *Sustaining Distance Training: Integrating Learning Technologies into the Fabric of the Enterprise.* San Francisco: Jossey-Bass, 2001.

Collision, George, Elbaum, Bonnie, Haavind, Sarah, & Tinker, Robert. *Facilitating Online Learning: Effective Strategies for Moderators.* Madison, WI: Atwood Publishing, 2000. www.concord.org.

Hoffman, Jennifer. *The Synchronous Trainer's Survival Guide.* Contact author at 860–767–0215 or see www.insynctraining.com.

Salmon, Gilly. *E-Moderating: The Key to Teaching and Learning Online.* London: Kogan-Page, 2000. http://oubs.open.ac.uk/e-moderating/

CHAMPIONS

Strategies for Leading the Change

Whatever your role—trainer, instructional designer, or training manager—in helping introduce e-learning in your organization, you will probably be fostering substantive change. Re-jigging an organization for e-learning changes the way learners learn, instructors teach, designers develop, and managers manage. It is no wonder you may experience considerable resistance. e-Learning normally means using the Web, CBT, and EPSS instead of attending classes, which is an adjustment—especially for learners. You need to use a wide range of thoughtful tactics to create a positive environment when you introduce e-learning.

You will gain greater understanding and obtain better results from e-learning from using the tips in this chapter. You will be more successful when championing e-learning, managing change, managing risks, and leading consultants—and get the most from consultants.

Championing e-Learning

"Don't forget, organizations are made up of people. People resist change. You need to deal with their resistance when you introduce e-learning."
—e-Learning manager

No matter how progressive they claim to be, organizations are always resistant to change, so you should not expect the dynamic to be any different as e-learning is introduced. Every new idea needs a champion. Champions play important roles in helping organizations understand new ideas. A champion needs to have in-depth knowledge of the ideas he or she is advocating and an understanding of the biases of those who are resisting. e-Learning champions know how to address management concerns and can deal with the effects of past e-learning efforts that failed or other issues that may arise during the training needs analysis phase.

A number of skills are required to start and to champion an e-learning project successfully. Among the most important are

- *Know the biases of the organization.* When approaching stakeholders with a proposal for e-learning, bear in mind that stakeholders might be skeptical about technological innovation. This might stem from involvement in a failed IT implementation or from another negative experience. An effective champion anticipates the resistance of stakeholders and develops counterarguments.
- *Remain positive.* Most people want you to succeed. They might lack the tools, the knowledge, and the structures to implement e-learning. Help them acquire what they need positively.
- *Be consistent.* When you lead an organization into e-learning, colleagues and clients will expect you to be predictable, dependable, and in sync with their behavior.
- *Bring issues alive.* The difference between a good e-learning champion and a great one is that a great one makes the issues come alive for people, creates a sense of urgency, and helps people sing from the same song sheet.
- *Use consistent e-learning terminology.* Teach e-learning terms to others and encourage everyone to use them consistently. A shared language will help people to understand what e-learning is and to communicate with one another.
- *Encourage frank discussion.* Dissension is not bad in itself. Create a safe place for opposing ideas to be expressed. Better to bring out and to try to deal with conflicting ideas than to force them underground to fester.
- *Be creative.* There is no one way to do e-learning. Find the approach that works best in your organization. Partnerships may be available to you.

Other trainers you meet or speak with at conferences or associations will be able to offer suggestions. And online learning does not have to be an all-or-nothing phenomenon. It can be combined with leader-led instruction.

- *Promote the program.* You will know that stakeholders are ready to embrace e-learning when they are willing to take the time to talk to you. Exploit these opportunities when they occur. Report positively on your progress and promote, promote, promote.

Table 9.1 puts these key skills for championing e-learning into check-list form. Use the checklist to establish the extent to which you and other potential e-learning leaders in the organization are prepared for this important task. If you (or your organization) do not have the skills required, consider training existing staff, hiring new staff, or engaging consultants.

TABLE 9.1. CHECKLIST FOR E-LEARNING CHAMPIONS.

Key Skills	Examples	High	Medium	Low
Knows the biases of the organization	Knows organizational history of techno-logical innovation; able to anticipate the resistance of stakeholders and develop counterarguments	☐	☐	☐
Remains positive	Able to help people acquire the tools, the knowledge, and the structures needed to implement e-learning	☐	☐	☐
Makes clear decisions	Able to make decisions and communicate them clearly	☐	☐	☐
Is consistent	Working style with clients and colleagues pre-dictable, dependable, and in sync with behavior	☐	☐	☐
Brings issues alive	Able to make issues come alive, create a sense of urgency, and help people sing from the same song sheet	☐	☐	☐
Uses consistent e-learning terminology	Able to teach and encourage others to use terms consistently	☐	☐	☐
Encourages frank discussion	Able to create ways for opposing ideas to be expressed	☐	☐	☐

Key Skills	Examples	High	Medium	Low
Is creative	Open to different approaches to e-learning; able to work comfortably with a variety of types of e-learning	☐	☐	☐
Promotes the program	Able to exploit opportunities for promoting the program and make positive progress reports	☐	☐	☐

Managing Change

Change management, like *risk management,* is an oxymoronic term. It's impossible to "manage" change in the classical definition of managing (planning, organizing, control). You don't plan change. Nor do you organize it or control it. But you can take measures to understand the processes of change, communicate these to people, and, most of all, keep people informed. Effective change managers do the following:

- *Deal with resistance.* A few people may resist what you are doing. Learn about them and the source of their resistance, which may be well-founded. Are they unwilling, unable, or unknowing? Develop strategies to deal with the causes of their resistance.
- *Communicate clearly, often, and decisively.* When you lead an organization into e-learning, colleagues and clients will expect the information you communicate to be predictable and dependable. Tell them what they need to know and be sure that your actions are congruent with your words.
- *Manage expectations.* Typically, at the outset of a large-scale change such as the implementation of e-learning, people are enthusiastic; later, when events don't go as well as predicted, when deadlines are missed, and when some unrealistic goals are not achieved, people may become edgy or negative. Manage expectations. Do not let people become overly optimistic at the beginning. This will reduce the likelihood that they will fall into despair when some target dates are missed.
- *Foster teamwork.* Effective teams—people helping each other—accomplish more than individuals. Members of effective teams place the success of the group above their individual success. Establish expectations for teamwork, model appropriate behaviors, and reward teamwork.

Use the checklist in Table 9.2 to assess the extent to which individuals in your organization possess the key skills required to manage change successfully. If your organization does not have the skills required, consider training existing staff, hiring new staff, or engaging consultants.

TABLE 9.2. CHANGE MANAGEMENT CHECKLIST.

Skills	Examples	High	Medium	Low
Deal with resistance	Able to identify sources of resistance; knows strategies for dealing with resistance or able to seek outside assistance	☐	☐	☐
Communicate clearly, often, and decisively	Able to issue predictable and dependable information; actions congruent with words	☐	☐	☐
Manage expectations	Knows how to deal with both overly enthusiastic and negative expectations and reactions	☐	☐	☐
Foster teamwork	Able to establish expectations for teamwork, model appropriate behaviors, and reward teamwork	☐	☐	☐

Managing Risks

We saw in our discussion of benefits, pitfalls, and risks of e-learning in Chapter Two that there are plenty of benefits associated with e-learning. There are also several risks. If you concentrate too much on the benefits, the risks might be forgotten. No one wants to be the skunk at the garden party—the negative person who continually underlines the risks! As an e-learning champion, you may not want to keep harping about risks, but you must keep them in mind. Understanding risks and how to manage them can help you to play an important role and to establish risk management procedures.

To practice *risk management* sounds solid, final, and effective. However, people who practice risk management use watered-down words like *minimize, mitigate,* and *attenuate.* Risk management is simply a matter of identifying potential problems, developing approaches to deal with them if they happen, and reporting on the status of the actions that were taken and their associated risks.

Leading Through Communication

One of the most important actions you can take in managing change and championing e-learning is to communicate effectively. This will help others to gain understanding and acceptance of your e-learning program. Think about how you would go about developing a communication strategy. Collect your thoughts around the following questions:

1. Who needs to know about the e-learning program?
2. What messages do various groups need to hear?
3. What should each group *not* hear?
4. When should the messages be delivered?
5. How should the messages be distributed?
6. Who should be the spokesperson?
7. Who should *not* deliver the messages?
8. What skills do you have for delivering the messages?
9. Where do you require assistance to deliver the messages?
10. Who can help when you require assistance to deliver the messages?
11. How should you approach people who can help you?

In the end, you don't really "manage" risks. All you can do is remain aware of them, take steps to reduce the probability they will happen, and lessen their impact if they do. A risk management strategy is an essential tool for e-learning leaders. Essentially, a risk management strategy consists of identifying challenges that could undermine the success of your project and meeting these head-on. It is best to record the risks and your actions in a regular, perhaps weekly, progress report that lists actions taken, helps focus your project management activities, and keeps everyone informed. A weekly report with risk management details will help to keep the project on track— or inform managers in advance that it will be impossible to meet deadlines.

Typically, risks in e-learning projects include delayed delivery of hardware and software, the unavailability of subject-matter experts to undertake specific tasks, slow approval of deliverables, changes to content, and expansion of clients' expectations. An effective risk management report indicates how theses risks affect the project, what is being done to minimize the risks, and additional risks that lie ahead. Four actions that will help you to manage risks are as follows:

- *Set up a thorough risk management reporting structure.* In your report, include the date the risk was identified and by whom, proposed mitigating actions, and a record of actions taken. Keep reports accurate and up-to-date.
- *Sustain momentum.* Every project has potential pitfalls in such areas as time, scope, quality, and resources. Monitor these four interrelated variables, report on their status, and develop tactics to attenuate risks.
- *Get early wins.* As you implement e-learning and incur problems and opportunities, go after the rewards that are easiest to harvest. You need some early wins to demonstrate success to others.
- *Manage scope creep.* As e-learning projects progress, expectations of people involved in the projects may grow. Most of these expectations can only be met by doing additional work. If you do agree to take on more than you outlined in your original work plan, be very clear about the requirement for more resources or additional time. If not, quality will suffer when you are forced to make do without enough resources and try to squeeze more work into the same amount of time. In addition, you might miss deadlines or have to compromise some part of your project.

Use the checklist in Table 9.3 to assess the extent to which your organization possesses the skills required to manage risks successfully. If your organization does not have the skills required, consider training existing staff, hiring new staff, or engaging consultants.

TABLE 9.3. RISK MANAGEMENT CHECKLIST.

Skills	Examples	High	Medium	Low
Set up a thorough risk management reporting structure	Able to keep accurate and up-to-date records, including date risk identified, by whom, proposed mitigating action, action taken	☐	☐	☐
Sustain momentum	Potential pitfalls such as time, scope, quality, and resources identified; able to monitor and report status continuously and develop tactics to attenuate	☐	☐	☐
Get early wins	Evaluate problems and opportunities, harvest easy rewards	☐	☐	☐
Manage scope creep	Able to manage expectations of people involved in project; identify and communicate clearly when additional work requires additional resources or time	☐	☐	☐

Leading Consultants

When faced with new challenges, new knowledge, or a shortage of resources, it often makes sense to hire outside consultants. (I say this as a former training manager who hired consultants to help my teams introduce new e-learning products and services and now is a consultant who provides these services to others.) Consultants can provide valuable help in developing strategies and materials for all four types of e-learning. An experienced e-learning consultant could help you understand the strengths and weaknesses of new approaches; assist you in deciding whether they are appropriate in your workplace; and provide information to help you build a business case for alternative, creative approaches to training and education. A good consultant will save you time and money by helping you to avoid failure.

> "Rapid changes occurring in the world make it almost impossible for the executive team to remain knowledgeable about their industry, remain focused on their customers, stay ahead of their competition, and know what to do instantly when these factors collide in a negative way. Consultants offer the knowledge, information, data, and systems to solve the puzzle.
>
> "As you might imagine, based on these trends, e-learning will be in great demand by clients. A consultant who can provide e-learning support will be very busy indeed! Consultants will provide the 'people power' that corporations will not have. They will also fulfill the leadership role for executives who do not have the knowledge, expertise, or experience with e-learning."   —Elaine Biech is a strategic implementation consultant and author of *The Business of Consulting* and *The Consultant's Quick Start Guide*

Choosing a Consultant

In the current context of cost cutting, innovation, and new training technology, it might make good sense to hire outsiders, but there is no magic rule. Selecting the right consultant requires that you plan your work and work your plan—patiently and systematically.

How do you learn what resources are available? Where do you look for help? How do you know when you've found a good consultant? How do you get the most for your money? Here are a few guidelines that will simplify your decision making—and make life a little less stressful.

Know What You Want. There are basically two reasons for using consultants. First, consultants are—presumably—professionals who have the specialized resources, skills, and knowledge required to do the job. Qualified consultants offer up-to-date information and fresh approaches for your training. Second, external consultants could help you avoid the often-substantial hidden costs of starting from scratch to design and deliver your own training. A consultant might have developed a CBT or WBT "engine" that is tested and robust—and available for you to use quickly. If your content fits into this engine well, your development costs and headaches (and support nightmares) will be reduced. With the bottom line in mind, bringing in outsiders may be the best way to ensure a quality product and to avoid costs associated with hiring or diverting staff to your e-learning needs.

Find the Right One. A large part of choosing a consultant comes down to common sense. Good consultants ask pertinent questions about your training needs, and they don't stop until they get clear answers. For instance, a training specialist or production manager might identify a need for an accident investigation course. A good consultant will help you determine your exact need. Is it for theory, investigation skills, reporting procedures, analysis, follow-up, or all of the above? A good consultant will "customize" the training by addressing your identified needs, using your accident investigation forms, tailoring examples and case studies to your workplace, and making sure the course achieves your objectives.

Quantify Your Choice. If you interview a few consultants or review proposals from several consultants over a period of a few days, everything becomes a blur and it is difficult to make a meaningful comparison. A simple rating guide can help you record your observations and compare candidates. Adapt the checklist in Table 9.4 to your specific situation.

TABLE 9.4. CONSULTANT RATING CHECKLIST.

Attribute	Does Not Have	High	Medium	Low
e-Learning experience in the particular aspect where you require help	☐	☐	☐	☐
Experience in your industry	☐	☐	☐	☐
Good references (that you have checked)	☐	☐	☐	☐
Availability at a convenient time for you	☐	☐	☐	☐
Good chemistry with people in your organization	☐	☐	☐	☐
Willingness to customize material for your organization	☐	☐	☐	☐
Knowledge of pertinent hardware	☐	☐	☐	☐
Knowledge of pertinent software	☐	☐	☐	☐
Ability to grasp your needs	☐	☐	☐	☐
Thorough approach to work	☐	☐	☐	☐
Reasonably priced	☐	☐	☐	☐
Articulate	☐	☐	☐	☐

Getting the Most from Consultants

Working with consultants means providing what they need to start and collaborating throughout the project to ensure that they receive what they need to keep working productively. The checklist in Table 9.5 combines tips for working with consultants with an assessment feature. It was developed from the experiences of e-learning consultants who worked with excellent managers and not-so-excellent managers. Use it to assess the extent that your organization has the ability to work with consultants effectively.

TABLE 9.5. CHECKLIST FOR ASSESSING THE ABILITY
TO WORK WITH CONSULTANTS.

Tips	Examples	High	Medium	Low
Know what you want	On some projects, consultants waste time at the beginning because the client has not decided what is wanted. Work out all the details of what consultants will be doing before they arrive.	☐	☐	☐

Tips	Examples	High	Medium	Low
Have resources ready	When consultants arrive on a project, they can become productive immediately if you hand them the materials they require along with a list of contacts, a schedule of meetings, a list of subject-matter experts who are available, the software, the hardware, and access to the computer system they will be using. If you are not in the position to provide this material on day one, then allocate a few days to come up with a written plan.	☐	☐	☐
Set up a system of regular reports	Weekly reports work well, indicating what was planned, what was achieved, and, if there are gaps, why they occurred and what can and will be done to prevent gaps in subsequent weeks.	☐	☐	☐
Communicate about progress made and status of the project	Make the weekly status reports available to everyone. Have meetings to bring people up-to-date and to review issues.	☐	☐	☐
Make the consultants responsible for finding solutions	When issues come up, have the consultants propose solutions and work plans.	☐	☐	☐
Be realistic about approvals	Expecting twelve people to sit with the consultant and approve deliverables is not reasonable. Designate a small group of people to sign off on deliverables.	☐	☐	☐
Don't complete a product in one language and then start on another language	The second language group will always point out errors in the first production, so dovetail the two productions so that the first one has the advantage of a review by the second.	☐	☐	☐

Who Is Doing What?

e-Learning projects are often shared between internal and external resources, such as consultants. This presents another opportunity for leadership. Your organization might, for example, contract with an ASP (application service provider) to provide training courses. In some cases, you would purchase a complete package; in others, responsibilities would be shared. When sharing responsibilities, it is extremely important to determine who is doing what. The checklist in Table 9.6 will help you do that. Although we have set it up for internal versus external scenarios, you could also modify this checklist for use when responsibilities are shared within an organization by groups such as IT, training specialists, and subject-matter experts.

TABLE 9.6. SHARED RESPONSIBILITIES CHECKLIST.

Administrative Activities	Internal	External
1. Set up the virtual classroom, including the LMS	☐	☐
2. Select software for the virtual classroom	☐	☐
3. Set up a Web site	☐	☐
4. Adapt existing and new materials for use on the Web site	☐	☐
5. Set up individual classes for specific courses	☐	☐
6. Set up links to online resources	☐	☐
7. Construct online quizzes	☐	☐
8. Upload teaching materials to the virtual classroom	☐	☐
9. Market courses	☐	☐
10. Select instructors	☐	☐
11. Train instructors	☐	☐
12. Register students in courses	☐	☐
13. Administer financial aspects of registration	☐	☐
14. Instruct courses	☐	☐
15. Provide 24/7 help to users	☐	☐
16. Track grades	☐	☐
17. Provide certificates	☐	☐
18. Activate/deactivate users	☐	☐

Administrative Activities	**Internal**	**External**
19. Help users get set up	☐	☐
20. Help and encourage students to set up home pages	☐	☐
21. Administer the program	☐	☐
22. Test technology	☐	☐
23. Evaluate the program	☐	☐
24. Provide activity reports	☐	☐
25. Maintain the program	☐	☐
26. Maintain the technical structure	☐	☐

Test Drive

Think about the following questions and collect your thoughts. Based on your experience, what do you think will be the challenges when working with internal or external consultants or colleagues from different groups within your organization? What tactics would you recommend to minimize the negative effects of these challenges?

VALUE ADDED AND PROVEN

Measuring and Improving Programs*

Evaluate. Evaluation. It's no accident that the root of the word *value* is embedded in these words, for evaluations are undertaken to try to establish the value of objects, service, and e-learning courses. Taking an organization into e-learning is a major undertaking. And e-learning can be expensive. It makes sense to establish the value before proceeding. You may have other reasons for evaluating e-learning, such as the following scenarios:

- Your organization has been using e-learning for a few months and you would like to get a handle on whether or not it has been successful. You've heard rumors one way or the other and wish to verify their accuracy.
- e-Learning courses have replaced conventional classroom classes and you would like to compare their relative costs and benefits.
- You promised that e-learning would lead to any time, anywhere training. Now you wish to determine whether it has delivered as promised.
- Management bought into e-learning because they were told it is 50 percent faster, 50 percent cheaper, and 50 percent more effective. You wonder whether there is any truth to these claims. An evaluation should help to shed some light on the answer.

*Portions of this chapter were co-authored with Dr. Ralph Kellett.

- Your organization has had a few e-learning pilot courses and now you are considering developing additional courses. Before you move ahead, it would be a good idea to know what level of success you have had with the pilots.
- You do things right. You know that evaluations are crucial to performance improvement. You always evaluate, so you will also evaluate e-learning activities. It's expected in your organization.

This chapter provides ways to measure the value of e-learning, with an eye toward improving it. After an examination of basic evaluation concepts, we will review two case examples: the first illustrates how the Canadian military measured an e-learning program and derived its recommendations for improvements; the second demonstrates the return on investment approach used by a large electric utility to evaluate conversion of CBT courses to WBT.

Evaluation Speak

If you work with evaluation specialists, you will come across some terms that are unique to the field or terms used in other fields that are used a little differently in the context of evaluation. These terms often turn up in sets of two: alpha/beta, formative/summative, and validity/reliability are good examples. Short examples of how these terms are used in an e-learning context are given in Table 10.1

TABLE 10.1. EVALUATION SPEAK IN E-LEARNING.

First Term	**Second Term**
Alpha: Alpha testing is used during the development of e-learning materials. Alpha testing is the first phase of validation, normally conducted with members of the development team.	*Beta:* Similar to an alpha test, a beta test is used during the development of e-learning materials. Beta testing is the second phase of validation, conducted by external reviewers, not by members of the development team.
Formative: Formative evaluation is conducted during an e-learning event; the results obtained may be used to make immediate changes.	*Summative:* Summative evaluation is conducted at the end of an e-learning event and is an evaluation of the entire program or event.

First Term

Validity: Refers to the extent to which a measurement instrument or test accurately measures what it is supposed to measure.

Second Term

Reliability: Similar to validity, reliability also refers to the accuracy of an evaluation instrument. A reliable instrument could be used in another situation and would produce consistent results when used under the same conditions each time.

Issues with Evaluation

The word *evaluation* sounds definitive. When you hold an evaluation document in your hand, you would like to be able to say with certainty that it is accurate. Is it? How do you know? What can you do to increase confidence in evaluation studies? Table 10.2 lists some of the significant issues about the accuracy of evaluation, along with a few suggestions of what you can do to build a credible evaluation.

TABLE 10.2. WAYS TO BUILD A CREDIBLE EVALUATION.

Issue	Action to Take
How can I be sure that evaluation questions will test what they are supposed to test?	Do a literature search to find a validated questionnaire that has been used for another evaluation. Have your questions reviewed by several people. Pilot the questions with members of the target group.
How will I know whether the findings are scientifically valid?	Researchers have developed tests to assess accuracy of results and predict reliability. You can read about tests online and/or you can hire a professional to develop or to assess your evaluation tools.
Should I take a "scientific" approach to evaluation as described above or should I conduct focus groups and do "action research"?	Both scientific research and action research have an important role to play in gathering data. Consider using both, collecting both quantitative data (numbers) and qualitative data (opinions).
How can I locate expert knowledge in evaluation?	Speak to evaluation experts at professional conferences or local colleges and ask them for an estimate about costs to conduct evaluation studies in your area. Ask colleagues in other organizations to refer you to consultants and other

Issue   **Action to Take**

resources. There are plenty of resources on the Web.
Consult them. If you have questions after reviewing
Web resources, pose them to an Internet discussion
group. Some Web resources are listed in Table 10.9
at the end of this chapter.

Areas to Evaluate

The Institute for Higher Education Policy (IHEP) developed an evaluation
framework for e-learning that is a useful overview of areas you may wish
to consider in your organization. In a review of the literature, IHEP identified forty-five areas for evaluation or benchmarks and grouped them into
seven categories:[1]

1. *Institutional support:* environment, policies, and technological infrastructure.
2. *Course development:* development of courseware.
3. *Teaching/learning process:* the art of teaching, interactivity, collaboration,
   and modular learning.
4. *Course structure:* policies and procedures, course objectives, availability of
   library resources, types of materials provided to students, response time
   to students, and student expectations.
5. *Student support:* student services, including admissions, financial aid, student training, and assistance while using the Internet.
6. *Faculty support:* activities that assist faculty in teaching online, including policies for faculty transition help, as well as continuing assistance throughout the teaching period.
7. *Evaluation and assessment:* policies and procedures related to assessment
   and data collection.

Validation of the Benchmarks

After the forty-five benchmarks were identified from the literature, it was time
to validate them against usage by leading institutions. The National Education Association (NEA) and Blackboard Inc., a widely used platform provider

for online education, asked the IHEP to validate the benchmarks for Internet-based distance education. Six institutions participated in the study: Brevard Community College, Regents College, the University of Illinois at Urbana-Champaign, the University of Maryland University College, Utah State University, and Weber State University. To qualify for selection, the institutions (1) had substantial experience in distance education; (2) were recognized as among the leaders in distance education; (3) were regionally accredited; and (4) offered more than one degree program via online distance learning. To ensure that a broad spectrum of higher education institutions were represented, the study included a community college, a comprehensive institution, a research institution, and a virtual institution.

The forty-five proposed benchmarks were rated using two scales: one for *importance* and one for *presence*. The results of the study revealed that the forty-five benchmarks could be reduced to twenty-four through reducing some and combining others. The final twenty-four benchmarks are considered essential to e-learning quality. They are listed in Table 10.3 in an assessment checklist format to enable you to review your own organization against them.

TABLE 10.3. E-LEARNING BENCHMARKS CHECKLIST.

Benchmark	Met	Not Met
Institutional Support		
1. There is a documented technology plan, including electronic security measures, such as password protection, encryption, and back-up systems, and the plan is put into action to ensure both quality standards and the integrity and validity of information.	☐	☐
2. The technology is reliable and as fail-safe as possible.	☐	☐
3. A centralized system provides support for building and maintaining the distance education infrastructure.	☐	☐
Course Development		
4. Course development, design, and delivery guided by minimum standards and learning outcomes—not by the availability of existing technology—determine the technology being used to deliver content.	☐	☐
5. Instructional materials are reviewed periodically to ensure they meet specified standards.	☐	☐

Benchmark	**Met**	**Not Met**
6. Courses are designed to require students to engage themselves in analysis, synthesis, and evaluation.	☐	☐

Teaching/Learning

	Met	**Not Met**
7. Student interaction with faculty and other students is an essential characteristic and is facilitated through a variety of means, including voice mail and/or email.	☐	☐
8. Feedback on student assignments and questions is constructive and provided in a timely manner.	☐	☐
9. Students are instructed in the proper methods of effective research, including assessment of the validity of resources.	☐	☐

Course Structure

	Met	**Not Met**
10. Before starting an online program, students are advised about the program to determine whether they possess the self-motivation and commitment to learn at a distance and have access to the minimum technology required.	☐	☐
11. Students are provided with supplemental information that outlines objectives, concepts, ideas, and learning outcomes for each course in a clearly written, straightforward way.	☐	☐
12. Students have access to sufficient library resources, which may include a "virtual library" accessible through the World Wide Web.	☐	☐
13. Faculty and students agree on expectations regarding time given for completion of assignments and faculty response.	☐	☐

Student Support

	Met	**Not Met**
14. Students receive information about programs, including admission requirements, tuition and fees, books and supplies, technical and proctoring requirements, and student support services.	☐	☐
15. Students are provided with hands-on training and information to aid them in securing material through electronic databases, inter-library loans, government archives, news services, and other sources.	☐	☐
16. Throughout the course/program, students have access to technical assistance, including detailed instructions regarding the electronic media used, practice sessions prior to the beginning of the course, and convenient access to technical support staff.	☐	☐

Benchmark	Met	Not Met
17. Questions directed to student service personnel are answered accurately and quickly, and a structured system is in place to address student complaints.	☐	☐

Faculty Support

18. Technical assistance in course development is available to faculty, who are encouraged to use it.	☐	☐
19. Faculty members are assisted in the transition from classroom teaching to online instruction and are assessed during the process.	☐	☐
20. Instructor training and assistance, including peer mentoring, continues throughout the online course.	☐	☐
21. Faculty members are provided with written resources to deal with issues arising from student use of electronically accessed data.	☐	☐

Evaluation and Assessment

22. The program's educational effectiveness and teaching/learning process are assessed through an evaluation process that uses several methods and applies specific standards.	☐	☐
23. Data on enrollment, costs, and successful/innovative uses of technology are used to evaluate program effectiveness.	☐	☐
24. Intended learning outcomes are reviewed regularly to ensure clarity, utility, and appropriateness.	☐	☐

Four-Level Evaluation Framework

Donald Kirkpatrick has taught us to think of evaluation on four levels: reaction, learning, behavior, and results.[2] Many training professionals use the Kirkpatrick model as their primary evaluation framework. Whatever evaluation plan you decide to use, the model is sometimes useful as a cross-check. Table 10.4 describes these four levels of evaluation and suggests when and how each might be measured.

TABLE 10.4. KIRKPATRICK'S FOUR LEVELS OF EVALUATION.

Type	Questions Asked	When	How
Reaction	What level of satisfaction do participants feel about the training, for example, with their ability to use what they have learned, the course content, approach, and instructor?	Normally at the end of a training event, but may also be conducted partway through an intervention	Often assessed with a questionnaire that asks participants to rate the course in terms of key criteria
Learning	Did participants learn what was being taught?	May be assessed throughout a training session or at the end	During the training, assessed by questions that instructors ask or online quizzes; post-course quizzes also assess whether learning occurred
Behavior (Use of What Was Learned)	Did participants use what they learned? (Learning may have occurred, but was it used on the job?)	Assessed back in the workplace after a course ends	By asking supervisors what occurred; by observing students at work; by reviewing the output of learners
Results (Impact on the Organization)	What impact has the learning had on the organization?	Measurement taken before and after a learning event; requires that information about performance of the organization be collected before training to establish a baseline	After an intervention, performance is again measured to establish any change

A fifth level of evaluation, return on investment (ROI), has been championed by many. We discuss one version of ROI in a case study at the end of this chapter.

Four Target Groups for Evaluation

Looking at evaluation another way, we could use slightly different approaches, depending on whether we are evaluating the experience of learners, instructors, developers, or managers. Table 10.5 outlines how different approaches to evaluation might be taken for each of the four groups.

TABLE 10.5. EVALUATION FRAMEWORK FOR FOUR TARGET GROUPS.

Group	Issues	Methods to Collect Data
Learners	What attitudes did learners have toward e-learning before, during, and after the e-learning activity? What knowledge, skills, and attitudes did they acquire during the training? How much did they participate? What was the quality of their participation?	Self-administered questionnaire before, during, and after the e-learning activities; analysis of course-participation reports; focus groups
Instructors	What attitudes did course instructors have toward e-learning before, during, and after the e-learning activity? What knowledge, skills, and attitudes did they acquire by conducting the training? How much did they facilitate or dominate the interaction? What was the quality of their instruction?	Self-administered questionnaire before, during, and after the e-learning activities; analysis of course-participation reports; focus groups
Developers	What attitudes did developers have toward e-learning before, during, and after developing e-learning materials? What knowledge, skills, and attitudes did they acquire?	Self-administered questionnaire before, during, and after the e-learning activities; focus groups
Managers	Were the training policies effective? How much did the e-learning program cost? How do e-learning delivery costs compare to conventional costs? Is e-learning any time, anywhere training? How smooth was the technical delivery of e-learning? Is e-learning 50 percent faster, 50 percent cheaper, and 50 percent more effective?	Review of Web site postings; individual questionnaires; focus groups

Obviously, there are many, many more evaluation frameworks that may be applied in any particular situation. The case that follows illustrates one approach adopted by the Canadian military.

Case 1: Getting Value for Training in the Military

In the winter and spring of 2001, a team of consultants completed a formative evaluation of e-learning in a Canadian military organization. The evaluation dealt with a six-week, structured, leader-led Web-based segment that prepared students for a residential program in which they learned military management skills. The evaluation was conducted while the course was going on, and results were made available so they could be used to make immediate changes.

The key questions addressed in this evaluation were

- Is e-learning an appropriate delivery method for the selected content?
- Is the courseware well-developed for e-learning delivery?
- Is the technology used for the e-learning component (for example, WebCT, Internet, laptops, and so forth) and the level of support adequate for effective e-learning delivery?
- Do the administrative structure and management support enable effective e-learning delivery?
- Are the instructors and organizational support staff well-prepared to conduct the training through e-learning?
- Are participants well-prepared and sufficiently well-informed to take training using e-learning?
- Are participants given all necessary support from their home unit/base?
- Do participants find the use of e-learning and learning at a home location to be advantageous from a quality-of-life perspective?

The Evaluation Plan and Information Collected

The evaluators used the CIPP evaluation model (context, input, process, product). In the CIPP approach, information is collected about:

- The *context* of the training (both before and during the course)
- The *inputs* to the training (for example, student and instructor preparation for the course)
- The *process* (for example, student and instructor response to the e-learning environment, study procedures, and so on)
- The *product* (for example, student success on exams)

Four data-collection methods were used: (1) written questionnaires completed by students and instructors before and after the training; (2) focus groups with students and instructors before, during, and at the end of the course; (3) direct observation during the training (monitoring of Web discussions, observations during classroom sessions); and (4) document review.

Findings and Conclusions

The evaluation in the military e-learning training program was primarily a qualitative, not a quantitative study. The evaluators were more interested in what people said than in the numbers of people making a particular statement. The numbers were small, in a statistical sense. A total of fifty-nine participants finished the course being evaluated. Just over half of them responded to all of the questionnaires. Focus groups were held with all the instructors, and individual meetings were held with two. The evaluators had the opportunity to meet with just two of the five groups of students. Moreover, they collected a large amount of rich information (Table 10.6). Students, instructors, and course administrators made many valuable suggestions for improving the course.

TABLE 10.6. CASE 1: EVALUATION FINDINGS.

Question	Findings
Was e-learning an appropriate delivery method for the selected content?	Yes, it seems to have huge potential. The potential is realized when courses are well-designed and instructors are trained in e-learning facilitation.
Was the courseware well-developed for e-learning delivery?	e-Learning requires more design time and some different skills/knowledge to develop materials than does classroom instruction. Therefore, an e-learning design and materials development expert with specific e-learning expertise should be assigned to assist.
Were the technology applied for the e-learning component (WebCT, Internet, laptops, etc.) and the level of support adequate for effective e-learning delivery?	The technology worked well. However, using technology rather than meeting face to face in a classroom demanded a significant adjustment.

Question	Findings
Did the administrative structure and management-support enable effective e-learning delivery?	Administrative roles were new, and people fulfilling them were learning as they went. Training should be offered to people fulfilling the administrative roles.
Were the instructors and organizational support staff well-prepared to conduct the training through e-learning?	No. Both require specific training in their new tasks and roles.
Were participants well-prepared and sufficiently well-informed to take training using e-learning?	No. Participants were missing some of the basic skills, such as how to use Adobe Acrobat Reader, and some did not have the basic knowledge and confidence to teach themselves.
Were participants given all necessary support from their home unit/base?	Home units and military bases were supportive.
Did participants find the use of e-learning and learning at a home location to be advantageous from a quality-of-life perspective?	Some did prefer to study at home. Others found that using e-learning required them to use the family telephone line when other family members wanted to use it. Problem!

The following case about measuring e-learning is from the perspective of the return on investment or ROI.[3] The story has two major themes: (1) the challenges faced and how they addressed them in developing the training and (2) the return on investment analysis. This is a simple version of how to make an ROI calculation.

Case 2: Calculating the ROI for Converting CBT Courses to WBT

Case 2 involves a team introducing WBT to a large electrical utility. When they were given the mandate, the e-learning leaders identified several issues.

Which Subjects to Include in WBT

The utility's stakeholders decided to convert the most popular courses to WBT. Training staff thus determined which courses had the highest usage during the prior year. Also, commercially available courses were used when they were less expensive.

How to Keep Costs Down

The most significant way to reduce costs was to convert existing CBT to WBT. Using commercially available products also helped keep costs down. Fortunately, experienced staff were available to help with conversion activities. The total cost to convert and implement Web-based training, prorated over the life of the courses, was just $104,467. Using experienced staff helped to curb costs.

Because the training organization operates on a charge-back basis, all salaries, benefits, supplies, and utilities had to be charged to the larger organization. Work orders were set up for each course to collect the costs of developing, managing, and offering it. Some twenty different activities were captured as cost items. Any materials or supplies purchased were also charged to the appropriate work order. The data gathered in this way was used to calculate the return on investment (ROI) for the training program.

To address potential resistance to delivery via the company intranet, learners were allowed the option of either studying the material in a classroom or via WBT.

To maintain tight security around the WBT modules, learners were required to use the existing stringently enforced computer security system. Initially, only people with user IDs could take courses. Later, access was expanded to accommodate designated employees without access to the system. They took their training with proctors who had user IDs.

Faced with approximately sixteen thousand PCs, four thousand Macs, and four hundred other work stations, stakeholders decided to support only PCs and Macs. There was a considerable spread in the power and capacity of the computers available. Management decided to target the higher end machines. Assessing the least powerful machines at 0 percent and the highest end at 100 percent, the cutoff was set at the 75th percentile.

Return on Investment (ROI)

The team's analysis established ROI at 1:9.45. In other words, for every dollar invested, $9.45 was saved. The WBT courses were largely developed from existing courses, which kept costs down. And of course, with costs limited to converting existing courses, costs were lower than they would have been if courses had been developed from scratch. Also, for the purposes of calculating ROI, employees' training time was not factored in because they had to take the mandatory courses in either case. However, students taking WBT modules did complete their courses in less time. Because this was directly due to the new courses, the savings were considered in calculating ROI.

Development Costs
The development team took 1,845 hours to develop materials in one period and 1,668 in another, for a total cost of $208,935 (Table 10.7).

TABLE 10.7. MATERIAL DEVELOPMENT COSTS.

Item	Units	Cost per Unit	Total Cost
Hours charged to the project from October 1996 through September 1997	1,845	$59	$108,855
Hours charged to the project from October 1997 through April 1998	1,668	$60	$100,080
Total			$208,935

The life expectancy of the course is two years. Therefore, the prorated annual cost is $104,467.

Calculation of Download Costs
Macromedia's Shockwave® plug-in was used to allow the use of both audio and video. There were 3,968 downloads of fifteen minutes each, charged at a rate of $75 an hour. The costs of downloading were calculated as follows:

3,968 15-minute downloads x $75/hr x 0.25 hrs = $74,400

Total Costs

The annual development costs plus the download costs totaled $178,867, as shown in Table 10.8.

TABLE 10.8. TOTAL COSTS OF E-LEARNING PROJECT.

Item	Cost
Development	$104,467
Download	$74,400
Total	$178,867

Benefits

The benefits of the intranet-delivered training were numerous. The buildings at each plant are spread out, and the plant sites are from seven to fifteen miles apart. In addition, some employees live far away from the plants. So the largest savings resulted from participants not having to travel to classes—whether next door or miles away. For employees to leave their work stations, travel to a classroom or learning center, and return to work typically takes thirty minutes each way. In addition, employees coming from hazardous material areas must don and doff protective equipment, so their time is almost one hour each way. Total savings for the e-learning effort are shown in Table 10.9.

TABLE 10.9. CASE 2: CALCULATION OF BENEFITS.

Item	Units	Saving per Unit	Total Saving
Travel time to training center at 1 hour per course	10,899	$75	$817,425
Time that participants spent in the classroom	9,279	$75	$695,925
Instructor hours	2,862	$60	$171,720
Input for training records	10,899	$0.50	$5,449.50
Total benefits (cost savings)			$1,690,519

Additional Indirect Benefits

Among the additional indirect benefits were the following:

- Nine hundred nineteen classes that learners did not have to attend
- Space was freed up for other uses

- Employees no longer had to wait until a class was available
- Employees could complete training when it was least disruptive to production schedules

Calculating the Cost/Benefit Ratio

The cost/benefit ratio of 1:9.45 was finally calculated as follows:

Benefits of $1,690,519 ÷ total costs of $178,867 = $9.45

Conclusion

In addition to serving as an outline for conducting an ROI analysis, this case illustrates that implementing e-learning is a matter of common sense. In this case, the project team placed considerable emphasis at every stage on tracking expenses, reducing costs, and developing workable solutions.

Resources for More Information About Evaluation

The Web abounds in resources for evaluation, some specific to e-learning. Table 10.10 lists some of these resources to help you start. A few Web searches will no doubt lead you to many others.

TABLE 10.10. WEB RESOURCES ON EVALUATION.

Source	URL
Criteria used by the Brandon Hall Awards to evaluate Web sites	www.brandon-hall.com/public/faqs2/index.htm
Article about evaluating e-learning from ASTD's *Learning Circuits*	www.astd.org/virtual_community/research/What_Works/e-learning/e-learning_main.html
Sample questions for e-learning evaluations from the National Education Association (NEA) and Blackboard Inc.	www.ihep.com/Projects.php?parm=Projects/Blackboard.html

Test Drive

Develop an evaluation strategy for an e-learning course that you have either experienced or are planning to develop.

CHAPTER ELEVEN

THE VIEW FROM WHERE WE ARE

e-Learning Today and Tomorrow

We have been observing e-learning from the perspective of both the past and the present. It is tempting to consider e-learning from a future perspective too. But the future is difficult to predict. There are plenty of examples from the past that remind us to be wary about predicting the future of new technology.

Examples to Stir Us

Some people embrace new technologies. Others reject them. Some famous nay-sayers from the past are listed below. They can provide some humor as we consider the possibilities for e-learning in our own organizations:

- In 1895, Lord Kelvin, president of the prestigious British Royal Society, predicted that air flight was impossible. Eight years later, two American bicycle mechanics showed they had the "right stuff" and flew at Kitty Hawk.
- In 1900, the Benz Company, a precursor of the maker of a car that many of us would love to own, predicted that the market for automobiles would be limited to one million. Why? Because only one million families could afford a chauffeur.

- In 1927, H.M. Warner, head of Warner Brothers' Studio, asked, "Who the hell wants to hear actors talk?"
- In 1943, Thomas Watson, president of IBM, proclaimed that "There is a world market for maybe five computers."
- In 1977, Ken Olsen, president of Digital Equipment, said, "There is no reason anyone would want a computer in their home."

It's easy to laugh at these off-key pronouncements. The bottom line is clear: it's impossible to see into the future. It is also difficult for people to accept a paradigm shift. Some people who resist change and can't see the possibilities of new technology have much to gain but, like the organizational leaders above, they are sometimes rooted in their paradigms and cannot see new possibilities.

Some opinion setters in the training world are predicting big changes as a result of e-learning. Diane Gayeski and Lance Dublin are certain that e-learning is revolutionizing learning. Gayeski, as quoted below, looks at it from the perspective of instructional design, anticipating the proliferation of "learn as you go" opportunities for corporate training and envisioning a new role for training professionals as "information systems architects." Dublin predicts that big changes in wireless connectivity will transform the way we "work, learn, play, and live our lives."

"What we're seeing today in Web-based training is only the beginning of a new era in corporate learning systems. With the advent of small wireless devices that integrate telephony, audio and video capture, GPS [global positioning systems], and computing functions, we're going to experience a whole new wave of 'learn as you go' solutions. But all of this will require more than new hardware and software: it will mandate an entirely new approach to what we've known as instructional systems design. Instead of the top-down 'clone the expert' mentality, training professionals will need to embrace a new role as information system architect—the person who designs the pathways and maintains the links for collaborative learning and performance."[1]

—Diane Gayeski, principal, Gayeski Analytics, and professor of organizational communication and learning at Ithaca College, an internationally recognized pioneer in interactive media and corporate performance consulting

---

"People often say that the 'killer app' for the PC was Lotus 1–2–3, for the Apple Macintosh computer it was desktop publishing, and for the Internet it was email. Well, it's looking likely that the next killer app won't be e-learning, as John Chambers, CEO of Cisco, predicts, but rather wireless connectivity. While in 1999 fewer than 1 percent of all wireless users accessed the Internet, it is predicted that, by 2005, 30 percent of all Internet traffic will be accessed by a wireless device [*source:* BT Cellinet, UK]. By 2002 there will be one billion wireless customers versus 500 million PC-based Internet users [*source:* Ericssion]. By 2003 there will be twice as many wireless phones as PCs and by 2004 40 percent of all e-commerce transactions will take place through wireless devices [*source:* Gartner Group]. Wireless connectivity is a truly disruptive technological change leading to a transformation of how we work, learn, play, and live our lives."[2]

—Lance Dublin, head of Lance Dublin Consulting,
providing specialized services to executives responsible for the
planning, development, and implementation of e-learning strategies

In the science fiction world, *Star Trek*'s Vulcans, especially Mr. Spock, had a nifty training technique: the "mind meld." Vulcans could simply touch their fingertips to someone else's temple and zap! They uploaded knowledge, images, the whole enchilada to another person's brain! With today's rapid rate of changing knowledge, Spock's Vulcan mind meld would come in handy in a trainer's toolkit, but it seems that we will have to settle for other approaches to take us into the future.

How far will e-learning take us toward making learning more effective and efficient? It is apparent to most that it has the power to take us some distance. But like the telephone, air flight, and a host of earlier technological inventions, it is impossible to predict precisely where technology-assisted learning will go. It's too dynamic to make hard-and-fast pronouncements. One thing is certain, however: the more you are willing to look into the future, the greater the likelihood you will not be left behind. Therefore, we need to think critically about e-learning.

Thinking Critically

One of my principal aims in writing this book has been to encourage you to think critically about e-learning. The more you know, the more you know you don't know. As Alexander Pope reminded us:

> "A little learning is a dangerous thing;
> Drink deep, or taste not the Pierian spring:
> There, shallow draughts intoxicate the brain,
> And drinking largely sobers us again."
>
> —Alexander Pope, *An Essay on Criticism* (1711), pt. II 1, 15

Our knowledge grows as long as we continue to question, think critically, try new things, and evaluate what we have done. Yet the quest for knowledge is both frustrating and fascinating. Readers of this book have vicariously witnessed some of the frustration in the failed e-learning projects discussed in earlier chapters. Perhaps you have had some first-hand experience with e-learning frustration.

The most important knowledge you can have as an instructor, developer, or manager of e-learning is knowledge about *yourself.* What are your strengths? What are your biases? What impact do you have on others? What are the gaps in your knowledge? What is the best way for you to bridge the gaps in your knowledge—in line with your preferred learning style? What is your personal capacity to learn about e-learning? What is your personal capacity to plan, manage, and market e-learning? What roles might you assume in the brave new e-learning world: learner, instructor, developer, manager? And now that you have read more about it, to what extent are you motivated to become involved in e-learning?

If You Had a Hammer

Bill Ellet reminds us in a timely article that books, videos, and audiotapes are effective, less expensive, and perhaps more efficient than their e-learning counterparts: "Using traditional training media has become a bit like smoking: you may do it, but you don't brag about it."[3] The point is that a solid business case has to be developed every time you consider e-learning. You must identify all the costs and determine whether your organization is ready for e-learning. Most of all, be certain that e-learning is an effective means to teach your topic. Don't overlook books, videos, and audiotapes. Remember that you can combine conventional learning approaches with e-learning.

> "If the only tool you have is a hammer, you treat everything like a nail."
> —Abraham Maslow, lecture to Graduate
> Psychology Club, Brandeis University, Spring 1966

Two Perspectives

There are two perspectives on e-learning: the *technology* perspective and the *learning* one. We have discussed the learning side in this book because of the shortage of well-designed e-learning materials. e-Learning developers need to sharpen their pencils. However, they also need to work closely with their technology-oriented colleagues.

Technology is cool. Technology is trendy. Unfortunately, technology can create a host of problems. We need to be realistic about the expectations we set for technology.[4]

The "learning" component of e-learning remains the crucial element. Concentrating on "e" to the detriment of "learning" is a colossal mistake. Certainly, technology is important. Inadequate technology produces inadequate e-learning. Low bandwidth, slow modem speed, and buggy software can undermine e-learning projects. However, if the technology is good and the design is inadequate, you still have inadequate e-learning. The best technology will not render a worn, turgid, content-centered course into a fresh, dynamic, learner-centered adventure.

The best e-learning marries the right technology to the right content and methods. Successful e-learning stems from a partnership between experts in learning *and* experts in technology. It takes an ongoing dialog. As technology develops, as we learn more about how to develop effective e-learning, educators and their techie colleagues must work together closely to succeed.

The word *learning* reminds us to concentrate on individual learning, human performance, and human relations—on people, not on technology.

The building blocks of learning are a logical flow of information, interaction, human contact, nurturing, and clear communication. Technology does not create these elements. Good instructional design does, combined with solid, interactive teaching.

Remember: Put people before technology. That way your e-learning projects will succeed.

Thinking Critically About the Right Stuff

Good decision making begins with thinking critically, collecting the right information, sorting it logically, and using it to make a decision. When you have thought through a decision, you are able to explain it to others. When you have used logic to arrive at your decision, you are able to justify it to others. When you can explain your thinking clearly and logically, you can become an effective champion.

Critical thinking is not the pursuit of information. It goes deeper than facts. It deals with making defensible judgments. A successful critical thinker is aware of the processes he or she uses to reach conclusions. A successful critical thinker is always willing to try new approaches to thinking through issues and situations. Critical thinking is a skill. It can be taught, or at least the process can be illustrated and the learner can decide to use it or not. It takes time, patience, and dedication to become an effective critical thinker.

Questions are a key element of critical thinking. Training developers, training managers, and others associated with e-learning must ask pertinent questions, collect data, analyze it, develop cogent arguments, and explain their conclusions to stakeholders.

A critical thinker is able to identify bias in people's opinions and to pinpoint a lack of logic in others' thinking and reasoning. A critical thinker identifies superficial thinking and commercial hype. A critical thinker bases conclusions on solid evidence, not on speculation. Practice your critical thinking by answering the questions below in depth.

Ten Questions About e-Learning

1. Is my organization ready for e-learning?
2. Are individual learners ready for e-learning?

3. What type of e-learning is best suited to my organization and to its learners?

4. Should e-learning be combined with other approaches, such as leader-led instruction, coaching, and electronic performance support systems?

5. Is it necessary to develop e-learning from scratch or can modules be purchased?

6. If developing e-learning in-house, what bells and whistles should be included?

7. If setting up an e-learning program, what software should be used to develop, teach, and administer the program?

8. If developing e-learning to teach workplace skills, what skills should be taught?

9. What techniques can an e-learning instructor use to enhance the effectiveness of a program?

10. How much should our e-learning program cost?

Hello, Yellow Brick Road

While I was finishing the manuscript for this book, Canada's Royal Military College, the equivalent of West Point, invited me to a planning session. The continuing education division was moving toward e-learning and had decided to bring all employees together to obtain their input. We broke into discussion groups and I observed behavior that augurs very well for the future of e-learning.

I saw workers at all levels taking this discussion about e-learning as an opportunity to ask profound questions about the products and services their organization should deliver. They were looking at e-learning as an opportunity to improve customer service. They saw e-learning as a vehicle to move into continuous process improvement. They saw e-learning as a springboard for launching new products and services. e-Learning could help them move toward a learning organization. In short, they saw e-learning as a key element in rejuvenating their organization. To improve the quality of their work. To improve the quality of their work *lives*. I was excited to see individuals passionately participating in the discussion and seeking new ways to improve their work and work lives through e-learning. They were looking for the yellow brick road in their own backyard. And based on their bright eyes, smiling faces, and raised voices—as well as the quality of their discussion—I'd say they were finding it.

Goin' to Kansas, Here I Come

For the next few years, it looks as though many of us will be like Dorothy in the *Wizard of Oz,* trying to follow the yellow brick road to the wonder and magic of e-learning. Many decent folks are trying to get on the e-learning road: learners, instructors, developers, managers, and vendors. The reward at the end of the yellow brick road should be learning—for individual development, for better job performance, and for the common good. Learning propels us forward as workers, societies, and humans.

But Emerald City does not hold the answer. Wizards won't help us find learning's Holy Grail either. We need people who take learners and e-learning back to Kansas, to the basics of life. To the nurturing of Auntie Em. The fun of Toto. The caring of the farm hands. The determination, honesty, and good sense of Dorothy. Learners, instructors, developers, and managers must work together to make e-learning effective. Like the straw man, the tin man and the lion, we need to rediscover our brains, our hearts, and our courage— brains to think critically about e-learning, hearts to seek the right approach to e-learning, and courage to take a stand for the right thing.

We hope this book helps you find Kansas—and happiness in your own backyard.

Test Drive

For Folks Who Take Pride in Being Critical Thinkers. Here are some suggestions for critical thinkers:

- Read Andrew Feenberg's article at www.tao.ca/wind/rre/0622.html.
- Select points that you agree with and maybe some you do not agree with.
- Determine what you can do in the implementation of an e-learning program to avoid the pitfalls that Feenberg points out.

For Doers. Some Web sites offer an opportunity to set up your own online learning site. If you have not done it yet, this is a good time to start. You can use Blackboard at http://coursesites.blackboard.com/.

For Keeners. Do both exercises. Learn more. Learn to reap the benefits and avoid the pitfalls.

GLOSSARY

Alpha test.　The first phase of validation for a system, normally conducted with members of the development team.

Application service provider.　Vendor who provides training courses. In some cases, they offer a complete package; in others, both organizations share responsibilities, in which case it is extremely important to determine who is doing what.

ASP.　See application service provider.

Asynchronous.　Not occurring at exactly the same time. People communicating via asynchronous means receive, compose, and send their messages when they deem convenient. Examples are discussion boards, email, and voice mail.

Bandwidth.　The amount of information that can be carried through a phone line, cable line, satellite feed, or other Internet hookup. The greater the bandwidth, the greater the connection speed, the more data received, and higher quality images can be sent over the Net.

Behaviorist design.　Learning design based on the presumption that human behavior is predictable. Behaviorist influenced training contains predetermined objectives for what is to be learned, as well as predetermined reinforcers when objectives are met. In the extreme behaviorist view, a teaching machine could be used to instruct and provide feedback when answers are right.

Beta test.   Similar to an alpha test, a test used during the development of e-learning materials. Beta testing is the second phase of validation, conducted by external reviewers, not members of the development team.

Blended learning.   Refers to combining the four types of e-learning and also combining e-learning and conventional learning.

CBT.   See computer-based training.

Change management.   An oxymoronic term, as one cannot "manage" change in the classical sense of managing (planning, organizing, control). It does mean taking measures to understand the processes of change, communicating them to people, and keeping people informed. Effective change managers deal with resistance and help people adjust to change.

CIPP evaluation model.   The name is derived from *context, input, process,* and *product.* In this approach, information is collected about the context of the training (both before and during the course); the inputs to the training (e.g., student and instructor preparation); the process (e.g., student and instructor responses to the e-learning environment, study procedures, etc.); and the product (e.g., student success on exams).

CMC.   See computer-mediated communication.

Computer conferencing.   Using a computer to send and receive text asynchronously via the Internet. Most appropriate for groups of fifteen to twenty. Discussion boards and email are primarily used.

Computer-based training.   In the 1970s and 1980s, largely text-based lessons taught on a computer, often following the model of self-instruction manuals. With the popularity of CD-ROM technology in the early 1990s, CBT took on a new life. What had been dull, wordy computer-based training was replaced by multimedia. Combining images, voice, and videos made self-study more engaging and more entertaining. The term *multimedia training* was used to describe this new approach. Today, either term is used to mean CBT with multimedia elements. One of the issues faced is how to design materials so that instruction is emphasized, not pizzazz. *Also see* Web-based training.

Computer-mediated communication.   A term sometimes used to describe an online discussion, especially in academic circles.

Critical thinking.   Making defensible judgments, not the pursuit of information or facts. A successful critical thinker is aware of the processes he or she uses to arrive at conclusions. A successful critical thinker is constantly trying new approaches to thinking through issues and situations. Critical thinking is a skill that can be taught—or at least the process can be illustrated. It takes time, patience, and dedication to become an effective critical thinker.

Design.   Refers to planning training materials by setting training objectives and other high-level planning.

Development.   Refers to the act of using the course design document to prepare training materials, complete with exercises.

Distributed learning.   Learning that is separated by space or time using any form of communication and any type of media. It can be the product of either training or education.

DL.   See distributed learning

e-Learning (electronic learning).   Training, education, coaching, and information that is delivered digitally. e-Learning is normally delivered through a network or the Internet, but it may also be delivered via CD-ROM. In most organizations, personal computers are used, but personal digital assistants (PDAs) and other wireless devices are increasingly being used. e-Learning includes multimedia CBT and other forms of technology-assisted learning.

Electronic page turner.   One of the issues that CBT, multimedia, and e-learning face is how to design materials so that instruction is emphasized, not pizzazz. In the case of the first CBT programs, some did effectively instruct, through presentations, application, and feedback, but others simply put information on a screen and hoped for the best. Learners sometimes were limited to reading text on a screen and selecting a button to advance to the next page. CBT programs like these were sometimes derisively called *electronic page turners.* (Putting similar listless materials on the Web gives birth to a new derogatory term: *html page turners.*) Adding color, sound, graphics, and even video to electronic (or html) page turners still makes them page turners. Also, the addition of menus and the accompanying opportunities to select content does not make a page turner into a successful instructional device. A thoughtful instructional strategy is needed to reap the benefits of technology-assisted learning and to avoid the pitfalls of mindless pizzazz and information overload.

Emoticon.   Different variations on happy faces that can be used to convey emotions, irony, or other affective communications.

Force-field analysis.   A process analysis tool developed by Kurt Lewin used in the e-learning environment to identify underlying forces that shape training and e-learning in the organization.

Formative evaluation.   Evaluation conducted during an e-learning event. The results obtained may be used to make immediate changes.

Hybrid learning.   Not one of the four pure types of e-learning described in this book. I include it here as a reminder of the prevalence of the blended solutions that are created from combining the four pure types.

Informal learning.   When a learner accesses a well-organized Web site or a focused online community and finds pertinent information. It does not include a formal instructional strategy. Conventional informal learning examples are books, discussions, articles, and ad hoc coaching.

Instructional systems design.   Often referred to as ADDIE, for *analysis, design, development, implementation, and evaluation.* These processes can become convoluted and self-serving, and some of the criticism aimed in its direction is earned. Complex ISD models can be counterproductive, but a simple ISD process with steps such as scope project, analyze, design, develop, pilot test, deliver, evaluate, and maintain makes sense from a project management perspective. ISD-driven training development takes time, but in the hands of a skilled developer, ISD gets results.

Interactive learning.   Much has been written about the virtue of interactive learning—using questions, exercises, and other activities to engage learners as active participants in the process. Interactive learning keeps students energized and helps participants absorb information and remember it.

Internet service provider.   A company or institution that provides Internet connection to end users. Provides an email address, connectivity software, and a set of modems customers can connect to and thus gain access.

ISD.   See instructional systems design.

ISP.   See Internet service provider.

Intranet.   A network of servers and clients within a single company or organization. An intranet uses Internet protocols and programs. Can also refer to that part of an organization's network located inside a firewall.

Leader-led learning.   Unlike self-paced, leader-led e-learning always includes an instructor, coach, or facilitator. Learners access real-time (synchronous) materials via video conferencing, an audio, or text messaging service such as chat or learners access delayed materials (asynchronous) through threaded discussions or streamed audio or video.

Learning centre.   A site away from the traditional workspace that employees can go to participate in e-learning in quiet and without interruption.

Learning management system.   An application, running on a server connected to the Internet, that provides a suite of capabilities designed to deliver, track, report on, and administer learning content, student progress, and student interactions. The term can apply to very simple course management systems or highly complex, enterprise-wide distributed learning environments. Examples include Blackboard, WebCT, and Sun's LearnTone.

Learning styles. People's preferred styles for learning. Teaching methods, whether in the classroom or through a computer, are most effective when instructors accommodate the preferred learning styles of the people being taught. There are many schools of thought about learning styles, and not one universally accepted approach to defining the styles or explaining how to adjust to them, nor does everyone agree on their degree of significance.

LMS. See learning management system.

Multimedia. Combining images, voice, and video for computer-based training. See also computer-based training.

Netiquette. Online "manners." The rules of conduct for online or Internet users.

Performance support tools. Online materials that learners access to gain help in performing a task, normally in software. The tool normally leads the user through the steps required to perform the task.

Plug-in. An accessory program that adds capabilities to the main program. Used on Web pages to display multimedia content.

Preferred learning style. The way that learners prefer to receive information or to absorb information. For example, some like to learn by doing. Others prefer to read or to discuss.

Reliability. Refers to the accuracy of an evaluation instrument. It also includes the concept that the instrument could be used in another situation and would produce consistent results when used under the same conditions each time.

Return on investment. Calculations of the benefits received from an intervention, training, for example, compared to the costs in time and money.

Risk management. A matter of identifying potential problems, developing approaches to bring them under control, and reporting on the status of the actions taken and the associated risks. Risk management strategy is an essential tool for e-learning management. It is best to record the risks and your actions in a weekly progress report.

ROI.   See return on investment.

Self-paced learning.   When learners access CBT materials, normally on a CD-ROM or over a network or on the Internet. Learners select what they wish to learn, when, and the pace.

SME.   See subject-matter expert.

Streaming media.   Refers to video clips and audio that begin playing seconds after a computer receives them from the World Wide Web. The media is delivered in a "stream" from the server, which means that users don't have to wait several minutes or longer to download multimedia files.

Subject-matter expert.   A term used to describe the resource person a training designer or developer consults to provide content for a training program or information to develop courses.

Summative evaluation.   An evaluation conducted at the end of an e-learning event to evaluate the entire program or event.

Synchronous.   Taking place at the same time, for example, using chat services or a live video connection.

Threaded discussion.   The communications between learners and instructors in leader-led courses via a delayed (asynchronous) means. These discussions are known by a variety of names, including forums, listservs, mailing lists, and computer-mediated discussion.

Threaded messages.   Provide linkages between email or computer conference messages so that readers are able to follow contributions to a single conversation.

Validity.   The extent to which a measurement instrument or test accurately measures what it is supposed to measure.

WBT.   See Web-based training.

Web-based training.   A form of computer-based training in which the material resides on Web pages accessible through the World Wide Web. Typical media elements used are text and graphics. Other media, such as animation, audio, and video, can be used, but require more bandwidth and, in some cases, additional software. The terms "online course" and "Web-based instruction" are sometimes used interchangeably with WBT. *See also* computer-based training.

Work analysis.   An umbrella term to include such needs assessment methods as job study, task analysis, performance analysis, and competency studies. All involve analyzing the job and the required levels of performance. Some look at the ability of individuals or groups to perform at the required levels.

END NOTES

Introduction

1. American Society for Training and Development (ASTD) and National Governors' Association (NGA) Commission on Technology and Adult Learning, February 2000.

Chapter 1

1. eTrainers course at the Masie Center, January 9 through 11, 2002.
2. www.internettime.com/e.htm
3. www.smartforce.com/cgi-bin/bvisapi.dll/cbt/build.000/trainer/default-user/implementing_elearning.htm
4. www.asymetrix.com/solutions/online_learning.html
5. www.cisco.com/warp/public/10/wwtraining/elearning/elearning.html
6. www.askintl.com/e-what.htm
7. www.internettime.com/e.htm
8. www.ils.nwu.edu/~e_for_e/nodes/I-M-INTRO-ZOOMER-pg.html
9. http://adulted.about.com/education/adulted/mbody.htm
10. www.ittrain.com/99oct/10–99-learning-feature1.htm

Chapter 2

1. From an email message to the author, Sunday, 14 January, 2001.

Chapter 3

1. Brooke B. Schaab & Franklin L. Moses, *Six Myths About Digital Skills Training.* Alexandria, VA: U.S. Army Research Institute for the Behavioral and Social Sciences, Research Report 1774, July 2001.
2. James Adams, *The Next World War.* New York: Simon & Schuster, 1998.
3. Anthony Kimery, The Wired Cornfield, *Military Training Technology,* 4(3), 1999, 10–13.
4. Roberto Suro, Army Plans New College Program to Aid Recruits, *Washington Post,* 10 December, 1999, A01.
5. *Wired News,* 15 November, 2001.
6. United Kingdom, Ministry of Defence, Modernising Defence Training, *Report of the Defence Training Review, 2000.*
7. Ibid, p. 32.
8. For more details on the nature and type of facilities required for e-learning as opposed to conventional instruction, see G.F. McVey, Ergonomics and the Learning Environment, in D.H. Jonassen (Ed.), *Handbook of Research for Educational Communications and Technology,* New York, Macmillan, 1996.
9. See www.nasa.gov for more information on this topic.
10. Kim Kiser, Operation Learning, *Inside Technology Training,* May 2000, 22–28.
11. Kristine Ellis, A Model Class, *TRAINING,* December 2000, 51–57.
12. See www.athabascau.ca
13. For more information on this topic, see the Athabasca University MBA Web site presentation entitled "Learning in the Classroom and Online—A New Look at Media Richness" at www.athabascau.ca/mba/.
14. Kim Kiser, Road Warriors, *Online Learning Magazine,* September 2000, 25–32.
15. Training's New Look, *The Globe and Mail Report on Education,* 5 March 2001, R17–18.
16. Lauren Gibbons Paul, American Express: Performance Under Pressure, *Inside Technology Training,* January 1999, 12–16.
17. For more information on EPSS and its benefits in the workplace, see Marc J. Rosenberg, *e-Learning: Strategies for Delivering Knowledge in the Digital Age,* New York, McGraw-Hill, 2001.

Chapter 6

1. William Horton, *Instructional Design for Online Learning*, from www.macro-media.com/learning, p. 21.
2. http://ase.tufts.edu/cae/
3. http://ase.tufts.edu/cae/
4. Mel Silberman, Why Learning Must Be Active, in *The 1998 Annual, Volume 1: Training.* San Francisco: Jossey-Bass/Pfeiffer, 1998, p. 269.
5. http://sstweb.open.ac.uk:8282/oubs/gilly/
6. http://sstweb.open.ac.uk:8282/oubs/gilly/
7. From an email to the on author Monday, 22 January, 2001
8. Marcia Conner, *Learning the Critical Technology*, Wave Technologies International, Inc., 1996, p. 15.
9. Contained in an email message to the author on January 16, 2001.
10. Mel Silberman, Why Learning Must Be Active. In *The 1998 Annual, Volume 1: Training.* San Francisco: Jossey-Bass/Pfeiffer, 1998, p. 269.
11. http://tip.psychology.org/sensory.html
12. http://www.ethoseurope.org/ethos/survey/vol2/teleet.htm

Chapter 8

1. Vicky is a pseudonym for an instructor at Michigan State University, East Lansing, Michigan.

Chapter 10

1. The Institute for Higher Education Policy, *Quality on the Line: Benchmarks for Success in Internet-Based Distance Education,* April 2000, www.ihep.com/quality.pdf
2. Donald L. Kirkpatrick, *Evaluating Training Programs: The Four Levels* (2nd ed.). San Francisco: Berrett-Koehler, 1998.
3. Based on the implementation of e-learning in a nuclear facility of 18,000 employees, www.astd.org/CMS/templates/index.html?template_id=1&articleid=23593

Chapter 11

1. From an email message to the author on Monday, 22 January, 2001.
2. From an email message to the author on Monday, 8 January, 2001.
3. www.astd.org/CMS/templates/index.html?template_id=1&articleid=24664
4. www.technorealism.org/overview.html

THE AUTHOR

Brooke Broadbent is the founder of e-Learninghub, an information and consulting service for e-learning. He helped establish the e-learning practice of a major management consulting firm and has managed all phases of a wide variety of learning programs in the public and private sectors, worldwide. He has taught online at eSocrates.com, Royal Roads University and Phoenix University. He holds a master's degree in adult education. Brooke is a frequent contributor to training publications. He lives in Canada, where he combines his love of nature, writing, and all facets of learning.

INDEX